Thinking of...

Building a Digital Operating Model with the Microsoft Cloud Adoption Framework for Azure?

Ask the Smart Questions

By Dan Scarfe, Sean Morris, Frank Bennett and Ray Bricknell

First Published in 2019 by 1 vision OT Pty Ltd trading as Smart Questions, Suite 3, 596 North Road, Ormond, VIC 3204, Australia
Web: *www.smart-questions.com* (including ordering of printed and electronic copies, extended book information, community contributions and details on charity donations)
Email: *info@smart-questions.com* (for customer services, bulk order enquiries, reproduction requests et al)

ISBN 978-1-907453-28-1

SQ-23-199-001-001

Smart Questions™ Philosophy

Smart Questions is built on 3 key pillars, which set it apart from other publishers:

1. *Smart people want Smart Questions not Dumb Answers*
2. *Domain experts are often excluded from authorship, so we are making writing a book simple and painless*
3. *The community has a great deal to contribute to enhance the content*

www.smart-questions.com

Reviews

Clare Barclay

Chief Operating Officer, Microsoft UK

"Building a Digital Operating Model with the Microsoft Cloud Adoption Framework for Azure" is a must read for leaders looking to understand how the rules of the game have changed, and importantly how to unlock the value that comes with the right model, great technologies and engaged people.

I love the fact it's practical and serves as a useful guide for those driving change and innovation in their business.

Evelyn Padrino

Azure Marketing Director, Microsoft

Adopting 'the Cloud' carries core changes for an organization, that go beyond the obvious technology aspects, incorporating business and process components needed for a successful digital transformation.

"Building a Digital Operating Model with the Microsoft Cloud Adoption Framework for Azure" provides a balanced and practical approach to operate in this new 'cloud era'. With its easy, and almost entertaining, prose, the book guides the reader through this transformation. Presenting insightful questions and 'real-life' references, it triggers internal conversations across the business and technology sides of the organization to identify and execute the right path for Cloud adoption.

Authors

Dan Scarfe

Dan is a passionate technologist and loves envisioning technology solutions that positively impact our culture and society.

New Signature is in the business of helping enterprise organizations harness the power of the Microsoft Cloud.

As EVP Global Solutions, Dan heads up the sales and marketing GTM vision conceiving new products and services which can help organizations digitally differentiate, working closely with the sales and delivery teams.

Dan has been deeply engaged with Microsoft's Cloud since its inception in 2008. He was advising Microsoft on Azure when it was still called Red Dog and has seen the platform evolve substantially over that time. He presents on this topic around the world and sits on the Azure Partner Advisory Council.

Dan has been involved in many start-ups over the years, some successful, some not, and does his bit through passing on lessons learned as a mentor within Microsoft for Start-ups.

Dan has authored two other books in the Smart Questions series.

Frank Bennett FRSA

Frank has a long career in Information Technology from the distant age of the mainframe and every evolution preceding the Cloud era.

He is Smart Questions' most prolific author with eight published titles. As well as writing about Cloud computing he is a practitioner and recently co-founded a Software as a Service business to assist charities and not-for-profit organizations with the improvement of their governance.

He is a mentor to Microsoft ScaleUp London. An independent expert on the European Union's Horizon 2020 CloudWatch2 program. He is attributed as the inventor of Market Readiness Levels and their conjoining with Technology Readiness Levels. In 2018 he gifted the invention to Oxford University Innovations for use by Research & Innovation projects in academia.

Now with a portfolio career he holds the Financial Times Non-Executive Director Diploma. He is qualified to advise organizations on the General Data Protection Regulation (GDPR) following completion of the GDPR Transition Programme at the world-renowned Henley Business School.

Frank is Deputy Chair of the UK Cloud Industry Forum. A Fellow of The RSA and Member of EY Independent Director Programme.

Ray Bricknell

With 37 years of international IT experience, Australian entrepreneur Ray Bricknell has been actively facilitating and commenting on the relationship between the mid-tier UK Financial Services sector and the UK Cloud Vendor community since 2010.

Ray's firm Behind Every Cloud developed the award winning and industry accredited Clover (Cloud Vendor Ratings) index. He provides advisory services to a diverse range of large and small clients from the Asset Management/Investment Management/ Hedge, Private Equity, Retail, Investment and Private Banking and Insurance. Formerly the CTO of an $8Bn listed Hedge Fund. Ray is currently Chair of the Cloud Industry Forum Financial Services Special Interest Group.

Sean Morris

Sean has been involved in the IT industry since the early 90s and has sat on both sides of the consultancy world as an in-house IT staffer and a consultant working for large systems integrators.

Sean has a background in professional services from working as part of an IT team for a top London-based law firm and in Telco working in Australia. Sean specializes in infrastructure services particularly around hosting and service management.

Sean runs a team of Cloud advisors and pre-sales consultants for New Signature UK, pretending he works for Dan.

Sean is passionate about the business of IT and the role IT can play in contributing to the success of organizations.

Table of Contents

Part 1 Business
'What the leadership team need to know'

Part 2 Technical
'What the technical team need to know'

Acknowledgements

We'd like to offer huge thanks to everyone that has helped and supported us as we wrote this book. The list is too long to thank each person, but particular thanks to:

- Mark Smith for championing this initiative inside Microsoft and encouraging us to do this.
- Stelios Zarras for your help and support along the way.
- Brian Blanchard and the rest of the Cloud Adoption Framework for Azure team at Microsoft for giving us the content to support this book.
- Evelyn Padrino, Pratibha Sood and Sonia Yu for supporting the new edition of this book.
- John Kendrick for sharing his valuable insights in the first story at the end of the book.
- Pete Gatt from Servian who contributed a huge amount to the thought around some of the concepts we describe, along with helping to write a good chunk of the book and sharing the second story at the end of the book.
- New Signature for giving us the time to write this book.
- Jane Scarfe for proof reading.
- Lara Scarfe for letting Dan spend endless evenings and weekends writing.

- And a final special thanks to our editor Adrian Chandler for tirelessly reviewing, tweaking, suggesting and making this book as easy for you all to read as possible.

Foreword

Mark Smith, General Manager,
Microsoft Solutions

We live in a time of unprecedented change. Digital and broader technology innovation are reshaping our world all around us.

The introduction of the Cloud and on-demand access to computing power far in excess of anything available to organizations before have turbo-charged this already fast rate of innovation and change.

In recent years, the Cloud has evolved from a set of technologies that augment mission-critical platforms, to become that mission-critical platform. It is no longer something used for lower impact workloads. It is becoming the central platform organizations are leveraging as the lynchpin of their digital transformation strategies.

As we hurtle along on this journey of change, it's sometimes difficult to give ourselves the time to take stock. To take the time to look back on what we have achieved. To assess what has worked and what requires more effort. To learn from others about their successes and failures. To understand and evaluate what good looks like.

This book seeks to do just this.

Embracing Cloud in your organization is more than just moving servers from on premises to someone else's datacenter. That part is the easy part. Fully embracing Cloud necessitates taking a long, hard look at your organization. What does digital mean to you? How do you go about digitally transforming your organization? What aspects of technology can you embrace to allow you to not only survive but also thrive in this brave new world?

This conversation extends far beyond the remit of your IT department. As leaders within your business, simply delegating the problem to IT is not the answer. Technology in itself is not the answer. The answer falls exactly between the traditional realms of business and IT. To truly digitally transform your organization your business leaders need to understand the role technology can play and imagine new technology-powered products and services. At the same time, your technology leaders need to far more closely align themselves with the business. It is these teams and these individuals who are uniquely placed to transform these ideas into reality.

The key to digital transformation is to seamlessly blend what we might describe as a business operating model with our traditional IT operating model. Only when these teams and these concepts truly combine can we be successful in this brave new world.

This book argues the need to establish a Digital Operating Model as this unique bridge between these two separate worlds. A seamless combination of business and IT operating models.

A combination of these two completely separate worlds is, however, fraught with difficulty.

The primary currency of a business operating model is agility. Business owners and business group leaders thirst this agility. They are often perplexed as to why things are perceived as being so difficult and time consuming. They are focused on customers and delivering them the capabilities they desire. Everything that gets in the way of this is unnecessary complexity and roadblocks.

The primary focus of an IT operating model is control. IT leaders wake at night worrying about availability, security and a raft of factors completely alien to the business. IT often shies away from innovation and change as it is often in direct competition with their driving goals.

This mismatch is one of the primary contributors to the "shadow IT" phenomenon of recent years. Business leaders demanding a level of agility not being adequately delivered by the IT department simply pull out their corporate credit cards and procure what they need, there and then.

Uncontrolled and unabated procurement of IT solutions is not a good long-term strategy. Control is still a necessity within larger, structured organizations.

A Digital Operating Model as described within this book seeks to achieve the best of both worlds. The agility demanded by the business with the control needed by the IT teams.

Preface

*Brian Blanchard, Sr. Director,
Microsoft Cloud Adoption
Framework for Azure*

We are living in the most innovative
era in human history. Developers are
delivering global user experiences,
creating and deploying applications
faster and at greater scale than ever
before. The value of data continues to
skyrocket. Those who harness data and AI are changing entire
markets. As markets change and expand, infrastructure engineers
are making businesses more agile and better equipped to capitalize
on change. Together, infrastructure, apps, and data are reshaping
businesses and driving innovation.

These changes, often referred to as the "Digital Transformation"
movement, are happening in every industry and every region of the
globe. The Cloud is a catalyst for this change, but architects,
engineers, and business leaders are the real source of this
innovation. They provide the human potential that is changing the
business world.

Harnessing this human potential requires something Microsoft
refers to as "Technical Intensity". Developing technical intensity
requires a combination of technical capability, technical adoption,
and trust. This concept hints to the correlation between cloud
technologies and rapid growth in innovation.

For decades, technical capability was constrained by a company's
ability to acquire hardware. The cloud has removed most of the
capital expense blockers to innovation, paving the way for technical
intensity and the ensuing innovation.

Companies that have most successfully driven innovative business
change have matched technical capability with an operating model
that encourages adoption of technology across the business and
customer base (Tech adoption). More importantly, those
companies have done so with sound governance and operational
management processes to provide safe guardrails (Trust).

This book builds on Microsoft Cloud Adoption Framework for Azure to guide customers as they create their own operating model for the digital era. This book and the supporting framework guide readers as they prepare the business, people, and processes to deliver tech intensity and lasting innovation.

Beyond the book: Microsoft works with a broad range of companies from start-ups to the world's largest enterprises. For years we supported companies as they delivered on cloud adoption and built their own operating models. Along the way, we've asked thousands of employees, partners, and customers about their experiences and best practices.

The Cloud Adoption Framework is a collaborative effort across Microsoft to demonstrate agile principles and a growth mindset. Together, we've learned from what works (and what doesn't). Together we've documented business, culture, and technology lessons that make Cloud adoption easier. The Cloud Adoption Framework is the output of those lessons, creating a collection of tools and documentation to guide companies through the iterative phases of the cloud adoption lifecycle.

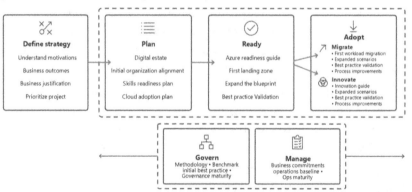

Making it real: Throughout this book, the authors link to various assets in the framework to guide you through your Cloud adoption journey. Those links and the authors' experiences come together in this book to describe a Digital Operating Model. The new set of rules. The new common environment where everyone can focus together on how to make our companies digital businesses. As you build out your company's Digital Operating Model, build technical intensity, or just deliver on a Cloud adoption project, we hope you will join us in expanding the Cloud Adoption Framework by sharing your experiences and feedback!

Introducing the Microsoft Cloud Adoption Framework for Azure

The world around us is changing at a rate none of us has observed before. The proliferation of access to scalable, pay as you grow, computing resources has changed the rules on creating new technology-powered experiences for customers. The rate of innovation continues to speed up every day, every week and every month.

But what should you do if this sounds like something you want to do? What does it mean to become a digital company? How can you leverage technology to differentiate your services in market? How can you prepare your people, technologies, and processes for this digital transformation?

An adoption framework is the lingua franca of all three major public Cloud providers in answer to these questions. Amazon and Google also both have their own adoption frameworks. Microsoft's adoption framework is the newest entrant and the authors would suggest the most comprehensive.

As Cloud computing has become mainstream it raises many questions and demands a framework for the resulting conversations. How do we create a digital strategy? What does that mean?

It is ultimately the myriad of decisions about how an organization's resources – technology and people – are organized to deliver business outcomes. Those business outcomes are defined and designed by decisions of people. And so, the Cloud Adoption Framework is a framework for people to collaborate and put technology to work.

It is unlikely that any one person will be an expert in all aspects of the Cloud Adoption Framework. Its application will involve the collaboration of a multi-disciplinary team. The purpose of this book is to provide the 'go to' resource for that team.

The Cloud Adoption Framework for Azure is divided into 8 sections:

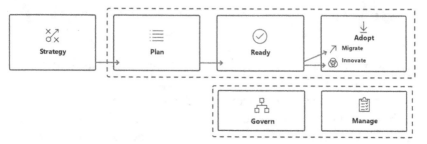

It starts with **Strategy**. What does it mean to be a digital company? Why is it that you are embarking on this journey?

It then helps you to **Plan**. What does your digital estate look like today? What is the make-up of your team today? What's the relative appetite for this change across the organization?

The next stage is to get **Ready**. You'll need to start to build out your base Azure environment. Think about how to structure it. Iterate and continue to add additional capabilities and services.

In parallel, it's vital you consider how you will **Govern** your environment. What are the key dimensions of governance? What controls will I need to put in place?

Once your environment is built and governed, you'll need to think about how you **Manage** it. What tools are you going to use? How are you going to operate it? How will Cloud plug in to your existing IT service management organization?

The final piece in the puzzle is to start to **Adopt** it. To start you might just **Migrate** workloads from on premises. In the future, you might be creating new digital experiences to help you **Innovate** and differentiate within your market.

A key differentiator in the digital age is developing a business culture that is agile. It is a culture that anticipates and feels at home with constant change. Those that have got to grips with implementing agile, report that it resulted in a shake-up of organizational structures. Mindful of that, it is recommended you read Chapter 5, so you are ready for the conversation.

The Digital Operating Model is where everyone comes together – Business teams, Developers, IT Operations. It is where discussions about 'digital at the core' of delivering business outcomes are turned into actionable plans. For some that will be the creation of a digital business. For others it may be a toe in the water with Cloud computing. Those organizations pursuing a digital transformation strategy will find the Cloud Adoption Framework is highly suited to the orchestration of that and we hope this book provides some context as you embark on your journey.

Who should read this book?

This book is presented in two parts.

Part 1 Business is for the non-technical reader, those concerned with shaping the organization.

Part 2 Technical is for the learned technical reader, those concerned with solving how technology supports the organization.

We encourage readers to read both parts so when non-technical and technical audiences come together there is a mutual understanding of what is on the mind of the other.

This book is about the creation of a Digital Operating Model. What we mean by that is how your organization consumes the resources of public Cloud-based services to compete in this digital age. In chapter 15 Funny You Should Say That, we have invited people who have been through the transformation to write up their experiences.

People like you and me

This book is aimed squarely at those who want to effect a change in the way IT services, and specifically Cloud services, are consumed and delivered to an organization. Those who recognize the vital role IT plays in a world that is increasingly technology-driven in what is commonly referred to as the 'digital age'. Those that want to become change agents. People like you and us.

This book is intended to be a catalyst for action aimed at a range of players inside and outside your organization. Here are just a few of those players, and why it is relevant to them.

The Board

The board has many things to consider. Every day, technology gets higher and higher on the priority list. With the rate of technological innovation and the pervasive use of Cloud computing it is a juggling act to not get left behind – never mind get ahead.

This book describes a model for how a business will make decisions to deal with ever-increasing reliance on technology. Those decisions are complex as they can conflict with the way IT is delivered today and previous investments you may have made. It's difficult to balance this with taking advantage of the innovation served up in the Cloud. Don't be fearful that you will drown in technical jargon. Part 1 avoids this and sets questions you will want to ask of yourself and others:

As you look forward, what technological capability will the business require? What skills and experience will you need in order to put innovation to work? Who do you partner with for knowledge and support?

Boards will be aware of the techno-political debate that places a new responsibility on organizations regarding the processing of data. A legal responsibility and accountability now accompany the decision to invest in technology such as Artificial Intelligence for the processing of data.

The connectedness and ease with which data can transmitted in the digital age, while creating new opportunities, also comes with new responsibilities. Data privacy has jumped up the agenda of politicians, regulators and consumers. In some jurisdictions, such as the European Union, the consequences of non-compliance are severe. Others are following. The California Consumer Privacy Act is expected to come into force on Jan. 1, 2020. This is a governance matter for the board's attention.

The CxO team

You might think that technology doesn't apply to you. It's an implementation detail within your organization. Something for somebody else to worry about. This is not true anymore. The discussion is becoming ever more complex as business and technology are interwoven and are core to strategy and execution in the business. Management has the ultimate responsibility for business outcomes and today's leaders must operate in the style of leaner ways of thinking and operating, as revealed in this book.

A measure of a successful company is the way it harnesses technology. That is both an offensive and defensive strategy. Our world has a long list of established businesses which have gone from glory to bust. Then follows the 'Oh poor them' analysis of what happened. We all know who they are – we used to shop there; they might have been a supplier.

So, if it is agreed that technology is now make or break then this book is for you. Engage the Board and Line of Business Managers in a discussion about what the business must be good at. That could be customer service, optimization of the supply chain, supporting a mobile workforce. These things describe how the business operates. This book serves up a discussion about how that evolves with technology and harnessing the power and innovation of Cloud computing.

CIO / CTO / CDO

You as the CIO, CTO or CDO are key architects of the transformation we describe in this book, and your role will change fundamentally. You're going to move from expert execution to expert orchestration and transformation. The execution of the Digital Operating Model is in your hands.

The Cloud Adoption Framework is your roadmap. You may want to align with partners who bring experience to your discussions, plans and execution.

Line of Business Manager

There are no better people to tell you about the demands of the business than those at the sharp end. You may hear that your competitors are delivering new products and services more quickly. Or it may be that they are making it easier and more convenient for customers to conduct their day-to-day business.

The availability of Cloud computing has created new opportunities for Line of Business managers to respond quickly. It is they who can equip their teams with new ways to deliver productivity and to work smart. That has served its purpose well and is now part of the big picture of how the business will create an agile posture to the deployment of technology.

How to use this book

This book is intended to be the catalyst for action. We hope that the ideas and examples inspire you to act. So, do whatever you need to do to make this book useful. Use Post-it notes, write on it, rip it apart, or read it quickly in one sitting. Whatever works for you. We hope this becomes your most dog-eared book.

Smart Questions

At the end of each part you will see a table of questions. Not all the questions will necessarily be new or insightful. The value you get from the information will clearly vary. It depends on your job role and previous experience. We call this the 3Rs.

Some of the questions will be in areas where you know the answers already, so the questions will **Reinforce** them in your mind.

You may have forgotten some aspects of the subject, so the questions will **Remind** you.

Other questions may **Reveal** new insights to you that you've never considered before.

We trust that you will find real insights. There may be some "aha" moments. In this context, probably the most critical role of the Smart Questions is to reveal risks that you might not have considered. On the flip side they should also open your thinking to opportunities that hadn't yet occurred to you. Balancing the opportunities and the risks, and then agreeing what is realistically achievable is the key to formulating an effective strategy.

The questions could be used in your internal operational meetings to inform the debate. Alternatively, they could shape the discussion you have with your IT vendors and their partners.

Thinking of…

Building a Digital Operating Model with the Microsoft Cloud Adoption Framework for Azure?

Ask the Smart Questions

'What the leadership team need to know'

Chapter

The Digital Age

Someone is sitting in the shade today because someone planted a tree a long time ago

Warren Buffett (1930 -), Businessman, investor and philanthropist

A new dawn

A ROUND the world the disruptive promises of the infamous dot com bubble of the late nineties and early noughties are finally being realized. The current generation of IT that had Cloud enter everyday vocabulary has businesses embracing digital transformation and digital-enabled business methods. As a result, a new requirement has emerged for a different kind of Operating Model – a Digital Operating Model (DOM). As we will explain, the Digital Operating Model is set to become the new lingua franca of business.

The work behind the Digital Operating Model where multi-skilled teams come together and collaborate is codified as the Microsoft Cloud Adoption Framework for Azure. Do not be confused, they co-exist. It is likely the CxO suite will be more comfortable to talk about the Digital Operating Model - it has a business ring to it. The teams tasked with delivering the Digital Operating Model will reference the Cloud Adoption Framework. More on this later.

The digital agenda is commanding CxO attention worldwide. Its outcomes will set the scene for high-speed business change over the next decade. This will spell opportunity for some and hazard for others. With constant change that appears to be accelerating new demands are put on organizations to respond.

The big shift is that organizations must develop a culture and competency to be agile. For some, particularly those bureaucratic organizations, that is a big ask. For this reason, we explore the balance between agility and control as a key theme in this book. We advocate the necessity of (some) sacrifice of control in order to enable the agility now demanded by those operating in a digital world. Moving the dial toward agility will please business teams. However, it will challenge IT teams accustomed to control as a doctrine.

A new day, a new way

One of the unforeseen side effects of the adoption of Cloud is 'shadow IT'. This term describes infrastructure and applications purchased or sometimes developed by the business without the engagement of the IT department. Why did that happen? Quite simply the Cloud served up new ways for business teams to get things done fast without the need to be (or engage) technologists.

Shadow IT supports line of business to move fast and gives them the agility to do what they need to do. It is also accounted for within delegated budgets and treated as an expense rather than an asset. Some say this has resulted in a loss of control of all-up IT expenditure. They claim that governance, standardization, economies of scale and overall strategic coordination suffer. Ho hum! Things are getting done and that's what matters most. Right?

New horizons

The prevailing best practice for centralized control of IT/business oversight is the formality of the IT Operating Model (ITOM). This is an aid to communication, coordination and control. Intermediary roles and translation functions like IT project managers and business analysts exist to define and agree the following:

- The requirements and priorities of the business
- The objectives and constraints before work starts. The budget and forecast future spend
- Formal plans and reporting for transition and migration
- Structured processes to align the goals and work, such as Waterfall and PRINCE2 ™ etc. Check out the Appendix for a definition.

The ITOM model can frustrate business teams' projects. There is always a queue of corporate priorities that are seemingly perpetually delayed. If they want results now, many have been tempted by the shadow IT option.

Shadow IT costs continue to skyrocket. In some cases, this can create data silos and system duplication. Yet still, it is no barrier to the insatiable appetite for Cloud – as we have witnessed through its meteoric growth. This has not gone unnoticed by the senior executive team and the Board. They want oversight as IT is a strategic resource. There is the hint as to why we wrote this book - *to be learned in ways to meet the challenge of aligning an organization's resources to grasp new opportunities of the digital age.*

As Cloud went mainstream a host of questions were initially raised.

- Can we really trust the safety of our data to the Cloud?
- Will we get locked into a vendor with no get-out route?
- What IT stays on-premises and what goes to the Cloud?
- Are the economics of the Cloud inferior or superior?
- Will the Cloud take away my job?

Depending on your point of view, these questions have been resolved. In any event, we have moved on.

The new questions are about how to harness the Cloud and not get left behind. For many that is in progress and adoption is growing rapidly - look at the success of Microsoft 365. Next up is how to take advantage of the continuous innovation in the Cloud. That is one important aspect of the Cloud Adoption Framework - putting innovation to work. The work ahead is to create an agile organization that puts it arms around the Cloud and each organization will have its own ideas about that. That will need context and we describe that as 'delivering your Digital Operating Model using a Cloud Adoption Framework'.

Disruption ahead?

Right now, business leaders are wondering what the future is for their own business models as evidenced below.

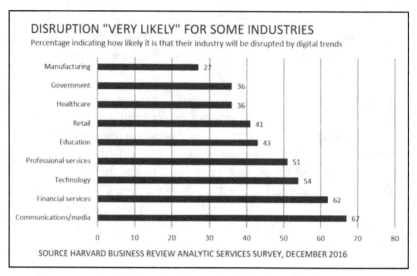

Figure 1 - Disruption by industry

Cloud technology enabled a wave of disruption and some sectors of the economy have had their business model disintermediated or destroyed. It all seemed to happen in the blink of an eye.

Some sectors (such as retail) are probably forecasting less disruption because they think it has already substantially occurred. Maybe they are right, maybe wrong. Others such as Financial Services (especially Banking and Insurance) appear to be bracing themselves for disruption.

Whatever lies ahead is going to result in change and there will be barriers. Of course, you can always bury your head in the sand but that could result in a bad ending. Alternatively read this book to kick start conversations and then get going.

It is a digital conversation

Many conversations are taking place, like this one:

Q. Do we have a digital strategy?

A. Do we need one?

Q. What do you mean by digital?

A. Well, it is something I am reading a lot about and it could be important to our future.

Q. What is it exactly?

A. Er, I am not sure. Who can we ask?

There is no recognized definition for a digital strategy; it is whatever is right and appropriate for your business. Many people are involved in the conversation and in consequence it can get ragged. You have probably guessed what is coming next. You need something to organize the conversation around. That something is the Digital Operating Model and the Cloud Adoption Framework. There, we said it again!

It is widely understood that a digital strategy is not an IT strategy. Do not focus exclusively on technology developments – although technology components will be major elements in the delivery of the benefits of your Digital Operating Model.

The challenge for many is to bring together the differing ideologies of the business and IT teams. Business teams seek agility to respond quickly to the external environment. IT teams do not always get that. IT teams seek control to cope with the complexity of IT environments. Business teams do not always get that. Both need to identify with something they can agree to coalesce around.

The new reality

The IT team is coming to terms with the fact that the control of their carefully managed IT platforms is too slow. The external facing business teams need agility for their 'digital at the core' competitive stance. The business is demanding speed of change, and the IT team is on notice to work with them to deliver that.

The writing is on the wall. 'We need a way to do new stuff together faster than before. We need it now!'

So, read on to learn more about why a Digital Operating Model is at the core of every successful 21st century business.

Chapter

The Digital Wave

The world as we have created it is a process of our thinking. It cannot be changed without changing our thinking

Albert Einstein (1879 - 1955), Theoretical Physicist

B USINESSES generally succeed because they continually evolve, although not always at great speed. Increasingly that is enabled by digital technology and talked about as innovation and transformation.

That occurs in a couple of ways:

- Take an existing business model and execute it in a better way than competitors. Deliver incremental improvements ideally at low risk and at low cost. Experiment and accept failure or hopefully succeed in your outcomes.
- Devise an entirely different approach to meeting customers' needs and disrupt the status quo. Figure out how to serve the under-served customer segment(s) with a complementary economic model and win big.

A business that delivers broadly the same as others and in the same way, might differentiate on service quality. It might offer improved speed or accuracy of delivery. It might have intangible metrics such as 'easy to do business with' or a strong brand image. The difference might often just be doing the same at a lower price. For established businesses a step change in the business model is typically harder to achieve than was bargained for. The process of delivering improvements is easier, but where that relies on associated IT upgrade(s) then it often happens rather too slowly.

That is the soft underbelly that the disrupter attacks as they move fast and often in stealth mode.

The D word

Talk about disruption conflates with new business models. They use technology to completely change how a product or service is served up to the consumer.

Three very well-known examples are Uber, Netflix and Airbnb. These three companies entirely changed the way their respective services were taken to market. The end customers' consumption was largely unchanged - it was the buy and fulfilment model that changed. These disrupters deliberately and intentionally attacked the established taxi, video rental and accommodation booking markets. Note that the accommodation booking market had previously been disrupted so the lesson there is – don't be complacent.

Whereas it was once the case that online was only for the brave owing to security fears (often hyped by antagonists), today there are very few businesses who don't transact online. You must also be exceptional, because other choices are just a click away.

This is today's agenda, as Microsoft report in its *Disrupt yourself or risk being disrupted: Competing in 2020* [1]

Will you be disrupted?

Business leaders know their industries are ripe for transformation and are eager to bring the benefits of technology to their business. In fact, in a new study by Harvard Business Review 'Competing in 2020: Winners and Losers in the Digital Economy [2], 80% of the 783 respondents believe their industry will be disrupted by digital trends. Most of those (84%) said their industry has either passed the inflection point of disruption or will pass it by 2020.

Digital leaders are doing today the things they need to do to be successful in 2020. Companies that form their strategies now, shift resources to new digital initiatives, and redesign their organization and culture will have a distinct advantage. Micro revolutions occur typically every 12-18 months, so companies must be in a continual state of transformation.

---

[1] *https://enterprise.microsoft.com/en-ca/articles/industries/microsoft-services/disrupt-yourself-or-risk-being-disrupted-competing-in-2020/*

[2] *https://hbr.org/sponsored/2017/04/competing-in-2020-winners-and-losers-in-the-digital-economy*

History is littered with the graves of businesses which, when facing a significant trend, made the choice to do nothing. They took the wait-and-see option. They either considered they were too big to fail or did not react fast enough. It is wise not be complacent.

> In 1965, the average tenure of companies on the S&P 500 was 33 years. By 1990, it was 20 years. It is forecast to shrink to 14 years by 2026. The FTSE 100 (London Stock Exchange) was launched in January 1984 and some 35 years later just 27 of its original members remain listed.

It is equally unwise to trivialize the decision. It is simplistic to assume or be bossed into blindly accepting that all businesses must disrupt themselves. Let's look at some very useful myth-busting content along these lines from the *MIT Sloan Management Review* [3] (Feb 06, 2017).

Myth #1: Every company should digitally transform.

Reality: Not every company, process, or business model requires digital transformation.

Myth #2: Digital transformation leverages emerging or disruptive technologies.

Reality: Most short-term transformational impact comes from conventional operational and strategic technology – not from emerging or so-called disruptive technology. That is to say, transform the basics before playing with the toys.

Myth #3: Profitable companies are the most likely to launch successful digital transformation projects.

Reality: If things are going well – crudely meaning wealth is being created for employees and shareholders – the likelihood of transforming anything meaningful is actually quite low. When existing market leaders drive disruptive technology, it requires a commitment from the top-down at every level. It may also require a significant culture change. At minimum, it will require a clear operating model to drive the digital and business change.

---

[3] Attribution: Stephen J. Andriole is the Thomas G. Labrecque Professor of Business Technology at Villanova University in Villanova, Pennsylvania

Myth #4: We need to disrupt our industry before someone else does.

Reality: Disruptive transformation seldom begins with market leaders whose business models have defined their industry categories for years.

Myth #5: Executives are hungry for digital transformation.

Reality: The number of executives who really want to transform their companies is relatively small – especially in public companies.

Author's remarks.

The consequences of 'do nothing' can be calamitous. Some boards consider it wise to elect a Digital Non-Executive Director to challenge complacency.

It is for you to decide if you believe that any of these myths characterize your organization's stance. Some businesses operate in a market that is highly susceptible to change. For them Myth #4 might be highly relevant. Transformation is easier in unregulated markets. Regulated markets are cushioned by the need for consultation and legislation. That can inhibit change. In that case, you have more time to anticipate and consider your move.

Intuitively, the answer for most must surely be: Keep a sharp eye on what is happening in your external environment (e.g. competitors) and hedge your bets.

The search for value

The things that qualify as 'transformation creating value' in businesses are often in the areas of cost efficiency and automation. Or they might lie in being able to offer the customer a more bespoke product or service. There are other ways that value can be created in this traditional scenario. All of them essentially come under the heading of efficiency – doing the same things faster, cheaper, or better than before.

What is different about value creation in a disrupter model? It is that it achieves a similar or better outcome to an existing business model in an entirely different way. Or it delivers an outcome not previously available. Such disruption is typically a step-change.

- Uber created an app for a customer to hail a taxi online. Almost instantaneously the customer receives information about availability and the approximate cost of the journey.
- Netflix delivered new release videos on demand to your TV. Bye-bye Blockbuster!
- Airbnb allowed a homeowner to rent accommodation direct to a guest. Some homeowners actually gave up their jobs to make a living out of renting a room. Wow!

Now that they are successful businesses, they have put others out of business, or at least made it harder for them to compete. Thought provoking stuff!

Few businesses choose to disrupt the status quo - until there is no other choice. Those that do are usually new entrants. Even fewer established businesses take the risk of disrupting the status quo by cannibalizing their core business. Other times, what is labelled disruptive is just fixing something that was badly broken anyway.

Talking business models

The business model is the new challenger ground. The disrupter starts with a blank sheet of paper. That gives them an advantage over an established business that has many things to consider before they disturb their business model. Both have readily available high-speed scalable and 'affordable' Cloud compute resources. So now business models are under threat from technology enabled disruption – and you don't need big bucks to get started.

It is probably fair to say that, in the case of most new entry disrupters, their business models have been entirely enabled by technology. Their definition of success is different. Starting from nothing and with very low costs they set out to win or steal revenue and to do it as fast as possible. They innovate fast to stay ahead of those who are better funded. They often end up being acquired by one of the incumbents they set out to disrupt.

Those hotheads with an idea working in a garage or a shared workspace are unencumbered by organizational politics and the other things that slow you down. They access high speed scalable Cloud compute resources and clever off-the-shelf code building blocks. Both are accessible on a pay as you go basis. This is probably the single most important factor in removing barriers to entry that previously protected the incumbent. Don't despair; there are also ways for established businesses to act as challenger. That is what Geoffrey Moore in his book *Escape Velocity* [4] calls the 'asymmetric bet'.

Today new entry disrupters don't need to read a book about building a Digital Operating Model. They are 'born in the Cloud' [5] and they know no other way. This book is primarily focused on the Digital Operating Model for the enterprise customer. Their situation has complexity by reason of their size, existing business model, and IT legacy. They have the most to gain, and maybe the most to lose.

Now, many of the business value improvements introduced into the enterprise so far have not been initiated by people whose core competency is technology. This is an important observation. These businesses have not historically been wired in a way that allows such a thing to happen.

Instead these changes are often inspired by a visionary business leader. It is they who drive the technologists and the other people in the business toward an outcome which they instinctively believe is achievable. They set the challenge. They provide the framework to facilitate the required change. This is often done by a mandate to copy or match a disrupter's new offering. Other times they are just making a bet. The technologists in the enterprise are then invited to respond to the challenge of delivering the what and the how.

Supercharge your BOM!

The Business Operating Model (BOM) is difficult to pin down. It's what you do and your unique differentiation. It describes how an organization is run and sustains itself in the process. It is increasingly reliant on technology. The technology historically sits with the IT Operating Model (ITOM) to support the organization's BOM and aims to meet its needs responsively and cost effectively.

---

[4] Geoffrey Moore is perhaps best known for his work 'Crossing the Chasm'. Escape Velocity is relevant reading in support of this book's themes.
[5] Born in the Cloud – a business that from its inception relies entirely on the Cloud for delivery of its products and / or services and customer services.

However, as more IT transitions to the Cloud then the ITOM has to evolve.

With the Cloud you can now supercharge your BOM and deliver a new level of agility with a Digital Operating Model as we describe in this book. The enterprise IT world is accustomed to a demand/supply model for innovation – the business demands, and the technologists figure out how to supply. When it comes to being truly innovative, this traditional operating model of Business-IT engagement has major failings. As the business world recognizes that disruption is probably going to be business as usual – the role of IT must change.

The IT team must become more entrepreneurial and innovative. It must develop a more detailed understanding of what differentiates the business that it is part of. It needs to start making suggestions about how to be more competitive. Sometimes it should come up with ideas for: 'We can save money by doing this better'.

Conversely, the business must get used to being receptive to new ideas. Some of these may be a little unnerving to live with. Artificial Intelligence and Robotic Process Automation are good examples.

Those enterprises that have moved into the world of the public Cloud now have new tools to apply to work. For example, the speculative processing of large datasets to reveal new insights for the business to act upon. It is now possible to undertake random experimentation on a whim that was not financially justifiable ten or even five years ago. Powerful stuff.

Put simply, it's reasonable to assert that business executives 'don't know what they don't know' about their business and the market in which it operates. This is not a criticism. It is just an observation. A trawl of LinkedIn reveals the insights of others on this point.

- *The truth is, if you aren't using data appropriately your competitors probably are."*
- *"Without big data analytics, companies are blind and deaf, wandering out into the web like deer on a highway" Geoffrey Moore, author and consultant.*

- *"It is important for marketing professionals to improve their skills in data analysis. It takes time and skill to determine which pieces of data are meaningful. But this process of boiling down data into consumable chunks is imperative for getting buy-in across an organization."*
- *"I hear this guy was pretty smart. At least that's the word on the street. But seriously, without the data to support a decision, too much is being left to opinion and chance. Why risk it? Test and Retest."*
- *"One of the toughest things to do with analytics is creating a narrative that is easy to understand for colleagues and executives. Obviously, we know that visuals are important, but it takes more than that to get the type of buy-in you want. When deciding which pieces of data are the most meaningful, start from the end and work backwards. What am I trying to achieve? What does the audience need to know?"*
- *"The amount of information available is overwhelming. So much so, that managers and executives don't have the time or ability to focus on specific data sets."*

””

The Cloud is awash with innovation and resources for a 'propeller head' (yes, some business teams still think that is what IT are, even though they are highly skilled, highly paid and high in demand). These folks are down in the basement ready to cobble together all the data that the organization has held for all time. Set them to work on that data – in the Cloud. They will throw it at a 'pay by the second' public Cloud data analytics platform and attempt to discover something completely new about the business that the leadership simply did not know.

For example; 'Did you know that our most profitable customers are not the ones we think, they are actually those that are …! Or; 'Our fasting growing client demographic is actually … - perhaps we should focus our marketing on that small but growing niche market?'

It is also now possible with the concepts of Agile software development and advanced coding tools, to test ideas quickly and at low cost. A failed outcome is acceptable as every outcome can be a learning opportunity. It is the new way and may feel uncomfortable at first. The IT team should be saying; 'Hey, we could knock that up on our website in a couple of weeks if you want to. Why don't we put it out there to see what happens?'

So, the lessons to learn from the business viewpoint are that:

- You DON'T have to be technical or understand digital jargon in order to be able to demand and achieve the delivery of value to your business in a digital age.
- You DON'T need deep pockets, simply access the economics of the Cloud.
- You DO have to create an environment whereby the seeds of such change are nurtured and encouraged.
- You DO need to set the conditions for your IT professionals to develop an entrepreneurial mindset.

In a digital age, technologists within an enterprise are key players. They must be fertile in thinking of ways to support the business to continuously innovate and work smart.

> Work smart in a digital age takes on a new meaning; blending a culture that promotes ideation with use of technology to test new ideas.

Why should so many of the highly disruptive ideas come from start-ups? There is no reason. The response of many established businesses is to create an environment for new ideas in Innovation Labs. That is the way to go, provided it is run with the discipline of a start-up! What does that mean? In the cloud! Work Lean. Work Agile. Readily accepting failure (no blame) and learning. Praise and reward the breakthrough.

People in the mix

The business that puts its IT in the Cloud can radically change with the overhead of operating IT substantially removed. This can mean fewer people are required and/or people with different skills are required. Then there is the need to consider what key roles are needed in-house to drive the Digital Operating Model forward.

This can present a dilemma as to who can step up to this role. Alternatively, do you go outside to find those skills? You can switch on technology really quickly, but the people in the mix require more time to come to terms with change and to acquire new skills and experience. With digital at the core of the Business Operating Model it is wise to keep a core tech competency in-house. This is a long game! We talk more about how to structure your teams in Part 2 of this book.

Chapter 3

The Way Ahead

There are no constraints on the human mind, no walls around the human spirit, no barriers to our progress except those we ourselves erect

Ronald Reagan (1911 - 2004), United States President (1981 - 1989)

I F only you could press the pause button as you ponder the seemingly endless assault of articles foretelling unwelcome news! They tell you your business model is going to be disrupted. They ask: What is your digital transformation plan and are you on top of your customer experience? The robots are coming. . . and. . . and. . . Oh! Then there is the 4th Industrial Revolution (4IR) characterized by a fusion of technologies that is blurring the lines between physical, digital, and biological spheres. (Isn't Wikipedia wonderful!).

There is a lot happening and much head scratching about what this all means.

We are in a time of boundless innovation and it can send the head spinning with questions about its relevance. Is it a fad? Will it pass? Many believed the Cloud was a fad – something that would peter out. How wrong they were!

Even so we are left with choices. Do nothing is always an option. Otherwise make a bet, preferably a calculated bet. Every industry has a predisposition to adopt technology, for example:

- The retail industry has bet on e-commerce. If you are a retailer today and not online then the future might be bleak.
- The automotive industry has highly automated supply chain processes and made extensive use of robots.

- The financial services industry, for so long rooted in conservatism, has its own FinTech innovation. They aim to compete with and disrupt long-standing (and some say, out-of-date) practices.
- Governments are not usually in the vanguard of technology adoption. Even so, they have implemented 'Cloud-first' policies.

Predicting the future is for the brave - or perhaps the foolish. The foundations of the future already exist. They are served up as the 4th Industrial Revolution and the technology drivers of that revolution are illustrated below.

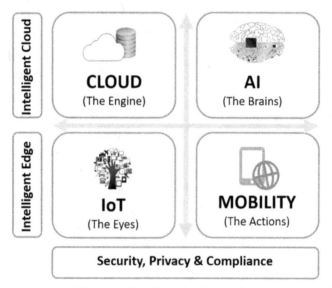

Figure 2 - The 4th industrial revolution

Notice that normal English words are written below the technology labels in the diagram above. For example, "The eyes" is under IoT: (Internet of Things). So now we have to think about what that might mean in a practical world. The quotation at the beginning of the chapter is especially pertinent.

There is great scope for creative thought to apply technology to work. In some cases, we now know that human work is likely to be replaced by a machine. The role of Artificial Intelligence with its human label, 'The Brains', is an example of technology providing both opportunity and dilemma. This has caught the attention of politicians because of the societal impact and ethical considerations. Microsoft's evidence to the UK's House of Lords Select Committee on Artificial Intelligence [6] is well worth reading.

Business leaders also face challenging times balancing the desire, or perhaps necessity, to put technology to use in a socially responsible way. If you think that seems odd, then consider the difficulties that Google [7] and Facebook [8] have faced from regulators and politicians. With technology so deeply ingrained in society it has come under intense scrutiny. With the growing use of technology there is a new aspect of social responsibility and ethical conduct for the leadership team to consider.

What lies ahead?

According to Professor Klaus Schwab, founder and executive chairman of the World Economic Forum and author of *The Fourth Revolution* and *Shaping The Fourth Revolution* (foreword by Satya Nadella).

> This Fourth Industrial Revolution is, however, fundamentally different. It is characterized by a range of new technologies (see diagram before) that are fusing the physical, digital and biological worlds, impacting all disciplines, economies and industries, and even challenging ideas about what it means to be human.
>
> The resulting shifts and disruptions mean that we live in a time of great promise and great peril. The world has the potential to connect billions more people to digital networks, dramatically improve the efficiency of organizations and even manage assets in ways that can help regenerate the natural environment, potentially undoing the damage of previous industrial revolutions.

This describes a revolution of great potential magnitude. No doubt there are consequences we cannot foresee. Does it all seem far removed from the daily grind of business? Your call.

You may have been an early adopter of Cloud or just getting started. The evidence is, Cloud is having a transformational impact on businesses. Cloud looks set to be the future direction of travel. How would you choose to talk about each of the technologies? How relevant are they to your future?

---

[6] *https://data.parliament.uk/writtenevidence/committeeevidence.svc/evidencedocument/ artificial-intelligence-committee/artificial-intelligence/written/69654.html*
[7] *https://europa.eu/rapid/press-release_IP-19-1770_en.htm*
[8] *https://www.ftc.gov/news-events/press-releases/2019/07/ftc-imposes-5-billion-penalty-sweeping-new-privacy-restrictions*

It would be a brave business leader to announce how they are going to deliver on the 4th Industrial Revolution. Maybe we should leave this to academics for the time being. Is it more realistic to frame that in terms of, as we describe it, a Digital Operating Model? Here is a reminder:

> The Digital Operating Model is where everyone comes together, Business teams, Developers, IT Operations. The Digital Operating Model is where discussions about 'digital at the core' of delivering business outcomes get turned into actionable plans.

Watch this space

The buzzwords 'Digital Transformation' and 'Business Transformation' are both popular. Both apply to the way businesses are reinventing the way they organize their work.

> **What is Business Transformation?** [9]
>
> Business transformation involves making fundamental changes in how business is conducted in order to help cope with shifts in market environment. (Source: Wikipedia).

Another point of view from the Global Centre for Digital Business Transformation report: [10]

> "organizational change is the foundation of digital business transformation"

That's because changing the nature of an organization means changing the way people work, challenging their mindsets and the daily work processes and strategies that they rely upon. While these present the most difficult problems, they also yield the most worthwhile rewards, allowing a business to become more efficient, data-driven and nimble, taking advantage of more business opportunities.

Turning ideas into action is what matters and this book serves the recipe. Who is on point for the transformation agenda?

---

[9] *https://www.weforum.org/about/the-fourth-industrial-revolution-by-klaus-schwab*
[10] *https://www.imd.org*

Executive Mandate	Line-of-business led	Built on third platform
• Digital transformation is at the forefront of customer conversations and is a board-level initiative. Executives view the path to capturing this opportunity as becoming technology-centric to deliver new customer experiences.	• Line-of-business (LOB) leaders such as marketing, operations, sales, HR and finance leaders are being called upon to drive business model changes and technology decisions, and to facilitate digital innovation toward a technology-centric business.	• The new generation of technologies - big data, analytics, social and mobile - are necessary to enable the achievement of a company's digital goals. These technologies along with accelerators like the Internet of Things (IoT) and artificial intelligence (AI), will dominate the unprecedented increase in future technology spending.

Figure 3 - Transformation agenda roles

At the front of the book, 'Who should read this book' describes the roles played by all those involved in the transformation agenda.

The idea factory

The new business dynamic favors building teams that are agile. They need a fail-fast mentality while keeping overheads low. The Cloud is highly suited to support this way of working. It is equally applicable to the micro business and to the Goliath. This is both opportunity and threat, particularly so for the Goliaths. Everyone will know a business that is a Goliath today but started out with just a few folks with an idea and a garage. In the same vein, some Goliaths that appeared permanent, have, er, gone.

New ideas are increasing translated into software and the Cloud has made that easy. You may have heard the expression 'Software Is Eating The World' [11]. It may sound exaggerated until you consider how dependent we are on software in our own personal lives compared to ten years ago. Not convinced? How many apps have you installed on your smartphone? In organizations, software is now the DNA – it is that important!

The Cloud serves up all manner of tools for transformation. You serve up the ideas and get down to work. The work is in your hands and the reference for organization of that work is the Cloud

---

[11] *Marc Andreessen* penned his famous *"Why Software Is Eating the World"* essay in The Wall Street Journal in 2011.

Adoption Framework. The Cloud is the factory floor on which ideas quickly come to life!

In the Cloud Adoption Framework for Azure Innovate section, there is guidance on how to drive business leaders to become citizen developers as part of an ideas factory. You can do that without dependencies on pro-developers until you need the scale, and the business models are all proven: https://aka.ms/adopt/innovate

Mission Critical?

Before riding off into the sunset; what priority should the transformation agenda be given? Is it mission critical?

Wikipedia defines 'mission critical' as: any factor of a system (components, equipment, personnel, process, procedure, software, etc.) that is essential to business operation or to an organization.

How do you begin to justify the answer?

Product development times are getting shorter. So too are product life cycles. The business model (the authors are fans of Business Model Generation [12]) must respond to competitive forces [13]. Innovation and the capability to react (get stuff done efficiently) must be incorporated.

Innovation points to: agile, Cloud, software, developers, talent, partners

React points to: Digital Operating Model, Cloud Adoption Framework, Agile, partners

It would be remiss, however, to overlook legacy IT. Legacy (or you may describe as heritage) IT will continue to support many vital functions. It is often the system of record holding vital data about finance, HR, and customers, to name a few. The driver for any discussion about technology is how it supports the outcome (profit, customer satisfaction, reducing supply chain costs, etc.). That drives the discussion to deliver the desired outcome with IT. Do you upgrade the investment in legacy IT and extend its life or go to the Cloud? No one size fits all! However, do think about the

---

[12] Business Model Generation at: *https://strategyzer.com/books/business-model-generation*

[13] Porter's five forces analysis at: *https://en.wikipedia.org/wiki/Porter%27s_five_forces_analysis*

platform that will take advantage of the technologies mentioned earlier.

This book is written for you whether you are either struggling with, or like the idea that Cloud is going to be the principal actor in support of the Digital Operating Model. The organizational capability you need is going to be different from that of the past. This book is not a textbook for the 'transformation' of a business. Rather it deals with the realities of a mega trend that involves a shift to the Cloud to access its raft of innovation.

Reality check

Digital is seemingly peppered in every conversation. When did you last create a new product or service and not consider what IT was required to support it? The digital part conversation has gravitated to Cloud computing and lays down a challenge to the past order of 'own and operate'.

Becoming a Digital Business

"Every company is a software company. You have to start thinking and operating like a digital company. It's no longer just about procuring one solution and deploying one. It's not about one simple software solution. It's really you yourself thinking of your own future as a digital company"

Satya Nadella CEO, Microsoft

It is hard to imagine an organization without IT. But how about describing your organization as a software company? Is it comfortable to a talk about your organization as a digital business with a Digital Operating Model?

- How do you feel about that?
- Is it alien or hard to accept as a reality?
- Are you ready to be fluent in this new language?
- If digital were core to your organization's existence, what would need to change?
- What is your capability to develop software?

For many the reality is past investments in IT will survive until it no longer serves its purpose. There may be justification to 'lift and shift' some past investments into the Cloud if that is the right thing to do. And sometimes there is no reason for change. The path to a digital business is going to be work in progress for some time to come.

We have moved away from thinking about data processing (hardware focused) and business processing (software focused) - and constraints. We have moved towards thinking about – ways to quickly respond to the changing needs of the organization - find the solution. That is the pursuit of agility. Then the conversation is about making it happen and that is framed in the Digital Operating Model and the Cloud Adoption Framework.

Chapter

Digital Countdown – The Race is On

By 2020 every business will have set out on a path to becoming either a digital predator or digital prey – which will your company evolve into?

Forrester Research

IT is generally accepted as truth that today technology supremacy creates competitive differentiation. It is also acknowledged that this is not easy to achieve. Cloud computing makes technology highly accessible and an economic alternative to the capital-intensive upfront cost to own and operate IT. Cloud computing is a now clearly a mega trend. [14]

Previously if your organization wanted access to innovative technology it had to write a big check and choices were limited. Now Cloud is a magnet for innovation and a shop window for software developers. It presents a showcase of technologies that are suited to organizations of all sizes. It is low-risk, with free trials and instantaneously accessible turn on-off compute and storage available. Cloud is the place to go to search for innovation.

Cloud is creating new household names. Some – you will know who they are – have risen to fame and fortune. For some, this mega trend has been a highly destructive force leading to the demise of organizations – you will also know who they are.

---

[14] Mega trends are global, sustained and macro-economic forces of development that impact business, economy, society, cultures and personal lives thereby defining our future world and its increasing pace of change.

You are a software business

That is not obvious until you think about the dependency on software and that is partly because it is invisible – unlike digital disruption. Many are now coming to the realization regarding just how important internal software development will be. In this context, software development includes Data Analytics, Business Intelligence, Robotic Process Automation, as well as other technologies you build yourselves. These will be key to the differentiation of businesses in the future.

A change is happening. With software readily accessible in the Cloud, the question being asked is: Why develop software in-house? We will answer that shortly. Cloud is serving organizations with just about everything needed for the *must do* things in business, such as running e-mail, accounting, Human Resources, Customer Relationship Management, and the list goes on.

Yet this 'go to the Cloud for everything' approach misses one major point. The Cloud is accessible to everyone and so creates a level playing field. That being the case, how do you then create competitive advantage through differentiation?

This may not be a concern. On the other hand, if software is going to be a core asset to your business and your Digital Operating Model then you will want more control of that. The previous chapter referred to every business being a software business. The interpretation of that is, software is the source for delivering productivity, efficiency and opportunities for innovation. With software at the core of a digital business – and growing in importance – what decisions do you face?

We are at the point of acceptance that almost all innovation will come from technology – and specifically from software development. So, isn't it now essential for a business to undertake at least a small amount of software development? Even if it is just to analyze what your data is telling you about the buying patterns of your customers, and deduce how to serve your customers better/faster?

It is not a fallacy to think that whatever business you are in, you are also a software business as software is Digital Operating Model DNA.

Buy, Build, or Both?

For a long time, there was a choice between two ways of acquiring software. Either you bought Commercial Off The Shelf (COTS) packages or *built* your own bespoke solution. We long ago developed in-house enhancements to third-party software. The *Buy and then Customize* option is really a special case of the buy solution.

The pros and cons of these alternatives have been much debated. We won't dwell here on ongoing software lifecycle costs and managing legacy. Now there is a new option: That is: No (or Low) Commitment Pay-As-You-Go software licensing models. SaaS provides a great starting point. Massive amounts of 'above the IaaS line' functionality has recently become available. This is a key feature of public Cloud platforms. The combination of these two elements enable what could clumsily be called a 'Rent and Configure the Building Blocks' model.

Suppose your thinking is to deploy public Cloud as a way to decommission your datacenter. In which case, don't overlook the opportunity to decommission legacy software. There is also the opportunity to change the focus of future development functions. Today and in the future in-house *coding* will be more like gluing together these off-the-shelf building blocks.

What is being done here is the orchestration of Cloud services with the implementation of the Digital Operating Model. To what purpose? Let's use a specific example.

The COO makes an ask of the IT team: 'I want to analyze a dataset and I need to know what it can tell me, and fast!'. The IT team take the dataset and clean it up inside Azure Data Factory. Then they put it into an Azure Data Lake. From there they build a cube to present it and visualize it using Azure Analysis Services. They then sit with the business lead and reveal the information (not *data*!) using Power BI.

This has been achieved using four different PaaS / SaaS services working in harmony and with nearly zero coding. The sum of the parts is completely customizable and tunable. Some of the language here is tech-speak. Anyway, now you know, you can impress your tech team! The point is that the IT team now have available the tools to rapidly respond to the asks of the business. Like?

This has huge implications as Microsoft now does the heavy lifting for you. New roles are created for architects and their job is to keep control of the plan for the *digital* house you are building. There are new roles too for business-savvy bricklayers who know how to cement the pieces together in order to extract value from your data - this is going to be a high in-demand skill!

We have described how the boundaries between IT and the business are being broken down. The purpose has already been called out – *agility*. How to apply this to your organization is for you to decide.

What is on the shelf?

Answer: Just about everything you can think of, and a whole lot more you didn't know existed.

The author's definitions are below, although there are more detailed (and technical) explanations at:
https://www.nist.gov/publications/nist-definition-cloud-computing

Software as a Service (SaaS)

SaaS applications revolve around user and application functionality. They are shrink-wrapped applications, delivered remotely, priced per user, and billed monthly. They typically provide customization and configuration options to allow you to align them to the demands of your organization.

They are though, by definition, pre-packaged. Not everything can be customized. They do have fixed, predictable costs and very little (if any) maintenance requirement. Office 365 is a good example. You bring the users. Microsoft does the rest.

Infrastructure as a Service (IaaS)

IaaS revolves around the server. IaaS has a lot of similarities to a traditional on-premises, virtualized environment. You can run servers in much the same way as you do today. The difference is that the server is in a Cloud provider's datacenter. The major difference from what you have today is probably in the level of automation and scripting made available. You also have, for all intents and purposes, unlimited capacity to create and delete virtual servers on the fly. You have complete control over configuring the operating system, storage, networking, and more. Think: Azure

Infrastructure Services. You bring the Operating System. Microsoft manages the low-level hardware and virtualization tiers.

Platform as a Service (PaaS)

PaaS revolves around custom-developed applications or application components. You can build an application by stitching together several platform services and deploying code on top of them. You have complete control at the application level, i.e. what the app is and how it functions. But you have less control of the mechanics of how that application is deployed and managed. The Cloud vendor does that for you. This also means you have less to maintain, support, and worry about. Think of Azure platform services such as SQL Azure and Azure Kubernetes Service. You write the code and deploy it as a managed application. Microsoft does the rest.

Functions as a Service (FaaS)

FaaS is an evolution of PaaS, with even less control, and even less management responsibility. It provides the ability to execute raw code as a service. With PaaS you still need to be aware of and pay for a (web) server, for instance. But you don't have to deploy it or manage it. With Functions, you just deploy your code block (sometimes called a *microservice*). Microsoft charges you based on the resource used each time your code executes. Think of Azure Functions. You bring the raw code. Microsoft does the rest.

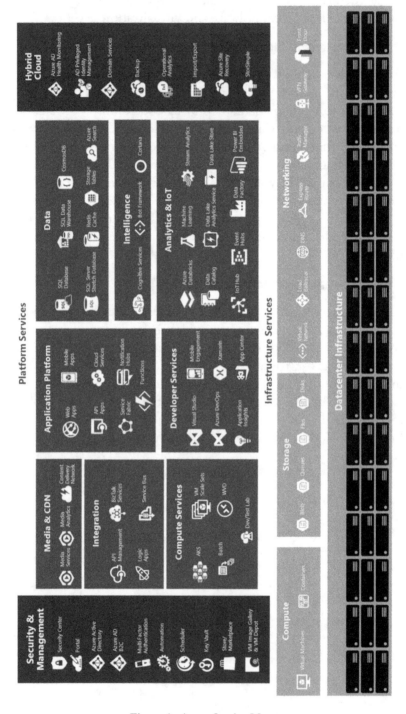

Figure 4 - Azure Service Map

What does this deliver?

FaaS is still relatively new. The three other services are extensively used today. In some cases, organizations have gone all in. They have completely removed their on-premises equipment, replacing it with a mix of these four capabilities. Those old server rooms have become meeting rooms! Or a higher profit margin.

Taken together, Cloud services deliver on-demand functionality. For example, they enable infrastructure to grow on demand and shrink on demand. You only pay for what you need. Previously such costs would have been absorbed as a fixed cost to meet the highest forecast volume of transactions. And then they would have been on your books for some years, irrespective of how your macro climate changed.

These capabilities can be exploited as part of an Agile approach to software development. They are for the creation of value and competitive differentiation. They are also the tools for the disrupter to go to work. FaaS moves us firmly into the future world of 'Cloud application engineering using microservices'.

Now is the time to press the pause button on tech-speak until Part-2.

Who controls the cost?

There is a widely recognized and obvious downside of allowing techies (and business people too) to have unlimited access to an on-demand Pay-As-You-Go computing resource. Business managers fear unexpected invoices for services, causing havoc for budgets and cash flow. This is probably right up there among their top three Cloud fears.

As a result, the emergence and adoption of public Cloud governance systems is vital. Organizations want to be able to budget for their projected consumption costs. They want to bill the time transparently to the incurring division or department. They want to pre-emptively sign off on limits and breaches. In other words, they want it to run in the same way as the traditional things that finance, IT, and the business have done (or wanted to do) for years.

Some organizations opt for a multi-Cloud strategy. Note the warning in Part 2 on that matter. Having made that choice, they need tools to help them pre-emptively determine the *best execution venue* for their production Cloud workloads. Later we touch on cost and quality governance in an Agile development world.

The business head conversation

A different focus is needed in the business conversation about adopting Agile development and using Pay-As-You-Go public Cloud services. This conversation must center on the view that the services described above are enablers for new ways to get ahead.

At the same time, it's vital to keep an eye on mega trends as they shape the world. The price of ignoring them can be extinction. Think about the retail businesses that ignored the trends for online shopping and on-demand movies? Some technology companies thought the Cloud was fanciful. They said it was nothing more than a return to the days of the mainframe. How wrong they were!

The business head conversation should not be wrapped up in technology. It should focus on staying relevant. In his book, *Hit Refresh*, Satya Nadella, CEO of Microsoft, calls out four initiatives:[15]

1. Leverage data to improve the customer experience
2. Support employee productivity with mobile collaboration tools
3. Optimize, simplify, and automate business processes
4. Transform products, services, and business models

Note how step 4 cycles back into step 1 in an iterative manner. Turning those initiatives into practical solutions is the next step. We now bring into focus some mega trends that are shaping and, in some cases, worrying society. [16]

---

[15] From Hit Refresh (ISBN 978-0-00-824765-2, page 126)
[16] The US Government set out its position in a paper (May 2018) at
https://www.whitehouse.gov/briefings-statements/artificial-intelligence-american-people/

Artificial Intelligence (AI)

It is early days for AI, but there are lots of examples that you may have already been exposed to. For example, have you visited a website and seen a pop up with a chatbot? That is a practical, basic use of AI.

Big Data (BD)

It is not often the case that we have too little data. More often there is too much to make sense of in order to provide the insights we seek. Somewhere buried in the data are nuggets of insight. If only they could be exposed. You could put people to work on what is frankly a thankless task. A better way is to use a computer to run *n* scenarios in parallel in a matter of minutes. That is *big data* at work.

Robotics Process Automation (RPA)

Factories around the world are advanced in their use of robotics. Now RPA is coming to the office where it can automate routine and repetitive human/computer interaction tasks. Insurance firms are beginning to staff the e-mail response agents in their call centers with robot-like software. This can read, process, and respond to common e-mail queries without human involvement. That is RPA at work.

Cloud is the enabler, and so building a core competency in Cloud is fundamental. The Cloud Adoption Framework is there to guide you. Be ready and prepared to use these capabilities when they become relevant to your organization. You are reading this book; you are on your way!

Now you may or may not be ready to put these capabilities to work immediately. Check out the noise with your familiar networks to gauge what is going on. You might not want to be "first off the block". On the other hand, last is never a good place to be.

Don't get caught out

The amount of data being created daily is truly astonishing. The Cloud has ample capacity to deal with this serving up massive on-demand computing power to store, index, and process. The pursuit of an improved business will necessitate finding better ways to process and analyze data. In short, finding ways to extract information from the ever-expanding data sprawl. There is no shortage of ideas for how that can be done. It is a big task involving more than just technical challenges. A more recent challenge is coming to terms with what you are allowed to do with that data.

As you investigate the possibilities to put the technologies referred to above to use, it is vital to understand regulation governing the use of personal data. In Europe the General Data Protection Regulation (GDPR) came into force on May, 25 2018 and substantially upgraded the rights of EU citizens (c. 513M) to control how their Personal Identifiable Information (PII) is used and curbed the freedoms of businesses to do as they like when processing PII.

There is a growing concern among consumers about how the personal data they share with businesses is used. Europe leads the world with its General Data Protection Regulation. India is seeking adequacy status (permitting the lawful transfer of data between EU member states and India) under the European Union's GDPR. Andorra, Argentina, Canada (commercial organizations), Faroe Islands, Guernsey, Israel, Isle of Man, Japan, Jersey, New Zealand, Switzerland, Uruguay and the United States of America (limited to the Privacy Shield framework) all have adequacy status (as of the date of publication of this book). The California Consumer Privacy Act is expected to go into effect Jan. 1, 2020. More will surely follow.

You will do well to tread carefully with the adoption of technology, such as Artificial Intelligence, for the processing of PII. Data can be stored, processed and transmitted anywhere in the Cloud. Your Digital Operating Model is not geographically confined, unless you decide that. So, always check compliance requirements with prevailing law/regulation. And do keep in mind that compliance is not globally harmonized. Don't stall out of fear, rather recognize the importance of due diligence.

On the one hand technology is becoming ever more capable of processing data and extracting the insights you seek. On the other hand, you are more tied as to how you are allowed to process data. If this is of importance to you then you are recommended to read the guidance [17] published by the UK's Information Commissioners Office (ICO) relating to AI, BD and RPA. That guidance topped the votes in the People's Choice Award at the 39th International Conference of Data Protection and Privacy Commissioners (ICDPPC).

Undercurrents

Technology is so ingrained and important to society that it is on the agenda of governments. This is a recent phenomenon. There is growing interest from policymakers in regulating the technology sector. At the same time, they want to avoid stifling innovation.

Should this put a stop to your plans? No.

The very institutions that policy makers work for, or are elected to, have similar challenges to businesses but on a much greater scale. They need technology to advance their work.

Even so it is wise to recognize that the techno-political debate is becoming louder. If you work in the media industry you will know that only too well. Keep a watching brief and talk to Microsoft. Because of their size and global influence, they are highly active in the techno-political debate.

You are a software business?

Driving the message of this chapter home:

- Do you treat IT as a priority for investment in the race to get ahead?
- Do you see value in building the capability to be a software business?
  (Software as the source for delivering productivity, efficiency and opportunities for innovation)
- Do you want to enable your teams to react quickly – to be agile?

---

[17] *https://ico.org.uk/media/for-organisations/documents/2013559/big-data-ai-ml-and-data-protection.pdf*

- Do you have in place strong governance concerning the processing of data?
- Do you know which partners you want to take on your journey?

We hope this chapter has elevated your attention to these things.

> The extent to which software development will differentiate your organization from your competitors will vary greatly across industries. It will depend on your value proposition and how software supports that. If you are in one of the industries most likely to be disrupted, and you haven't invested in Agile yet, you had better read on.
>
> The gun starting the race has already been fired!

Chapter

5

Agile – Small Word Quick Work

Perfection is not attainable, but if we chase perfection, we can catch excellence

Vince Lombardi (1913 - 1970), American Football Player

D EPENDING who you ask what agile is, they will tell you it is about moving quickly, or, they'll probably tell you that Agile (with a capital A) is to do with software development and that it's particularly helpful for software development projects with an innovation agenda. Both are correct. Here we refer to Agile. For the leadership team the thing to know is; if you want to be agile then Agile makes that happen.

The key difference between Agile and the standard coding methodologies for projects that preceded it is that Agile has as concepts:

- short term bursts (sprints) of coding
- regular face to face meetings (daily stand-ups)
- small teams that have a range of specializations
- test, fail quickly, avoid wasted effort and speedily change direction
- coordination of small coding activities in parallel (rather than big ones in a serial sequence – hence the dominant predecessor's name "Waterfall").

Agile has for the most part become the de facto mechanism for software development in recent years. You can do Agile coding without DevOps and/or Cloud. You can use DevOps and/or Cloud without Agile. They just happen to have evolved in broadly similar timeframes and they co-exist in an organization or a project very well.

It is not our goal to explain Agile development to you. What's interesting about Agile within the context of this leadership Part of the book is to explore its impact on the organization as a part of the IT Operating Model/Business Operating Model/Digital Operating Model discussion, and to position how Agile is about so much more than just software development. Agile and its bigger brother, Scaled Agile Framework® (SAFe®) for Lean Enterprises, are the glue that blends these three operating models together.

Why did Agile evolve into what it is today in the application development space?

Agile aligns today's software developers with the needs of the business that is continuously in search of innovation. It is fast. Much faster than methods used previously, and it is that speed that supports the business to respond to change. Whether that change is planned, or in response to external events.

We live today in a business world of 'accelerating change at an accelerating rate'. In this new world, horizon scanning and taking a long-term view of what innovation will keep the business competitive, is simply not viable.

The ability to react to the availability of new innovation and do so quickly is *as important* to being competitive as *the innovation itself*.

Read that again as it is fundamental to Agile's raison d'être.

Innovation in the Cloud is continuous and available to all-comers. In times gone by, those with the resources (deep pockets, skills) would outgun others. That is no longer the case. The competitive landscape has been levelled and actually tipped in favor of those that do not have the burden of legacy systems to maintain. Do you see the problem for some?

The central tenant of Agile is the backlog. Think of it as a long wish list. Every couple of weeks you pick new things from your wish list and deliver them. Because you only ever pick things off your wish list every couple of weeks, you can change tack much more quickly to respond to changes in priorities and external factors. The backlog is the central reason why Agile is so … agile.

Agile budgeting and forecasting

One of the biggest challenges with Agile is how you go about implementing it. Delivering small, discrete projects with Agile is relatively straightforward as it doesn't profoundly impact how you budget for these initiatives or require you to make wholesale changes to your processes. To truly embrace Agile, you need to make a few more major changes to the way you think about projects, budgets, and deliverables.

Traditionally, both the business and IT tend to think about IT projects through the lens of applications and projects. We need a new application, or we need to change an existing application, let's create a project and align resourcing and budgeting around this project. This is the wrong approach.

Instead, organizations that are truly embracing an Agile approach are doing things a bit differently. Instead of applications and projects, start to think about the notion of a product. This may be an internal or external product. Drop the functional specifications and handoffs between business and IT.

Instead, assemble a cross-functional team, comprising business experts, developers and other members of the organization in one cohesive, stable unit. Cross the business and IT chasm.

A large medical-device manufacturer significantly shortened it's time to market by refining its organizational structure. Under its traditional structure, there could be as many as 20 handoffs when a business unit shared its specifications and requirements with the technology organization for a new piece of software or an additional feature in existing software. Because of the interdependencies among its products, leadership knew it wouldn't be enough to deploy agile within one business unit or within certain product-management teams in the technology organization. In 2015, the company tweaked its product-ownership model so that software requirements were directly transmitted from dedicated product owners in the business units to the agile teams, rather than passing through multiple parties. With the change, the company was able to reduce the amount of time it took to release products in the market. The structural changes also facilitated the rise of several communities of practice. These role-based or topic-based groups (sometimes called guilds) are critical in agile-at-scale environments. [18]

---

[18] *https://www.mckinsey.com/business-functions/digital-mckinsey/our-insights/an-operating-model-for-company-wide-agile-development*

Getting the team structure right and changing the culture is but one aspect of the transformation you must go through. One of the most difficult changes to navigate is that of budgeting and financial planning. Historically, IT budgets were set every year and there were often painful trade-offs between different projects and initiatives the businesses were driving IT to deliver. Instead, align these budgets to these product domains and empower product owners to direct this funding throughout the budgeting cycle, having regards to changing business priorities.

The Disciplined Agile Consortium [19] has lots of great content to help with formalizing this budgeting process:

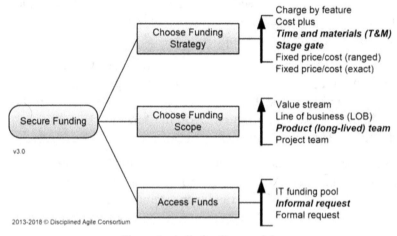

Figure 5 - Agile funding models

An interesting concept which is becoming more prevalent is the concept of venture-funding product development internally. In the same way a team of entrepreneurs might approach external parties to fund new products and services, now internal teams can vie for funding from internal investors. Initial funding might cover an MVP and then, directly linked to the success of the product with employees or customers, additional funding can be made available. This interesting approach laser-focusses budget in line with success and therefore significantly reduces wasted expenditure and cuts development running out of control.

---

[19] *http://www.disciplinedagiledelivery.com/secure-funding/*

Whatever approach you take to Agile budgeting and planning, ensure you major on flexibility and adaptability, whilst maintaining close visibility and overall control of your all-up spend.

Agile for the Enterprise

Agile is about so much more than just software development though. Agile has started to permeate just about every part of the business and has become a useful tool to manage almost any project you might want to run. What's interesting is how Agile can become the mechanism you use to run your most important project of all - your Digital Operating Model. This is where SAFe® comes in.

So, what is SAFe®? Several years ago, Dean Leffingwell wrote a book called *Agile Software Requirements* [20]. It became a best-seller that gave the world its first glimpse of what would eventually be known as SAFe®. It described a framework – called the "Agile Enterprise Big Picture" – that visualized how to apply Lean and Agile practices and principles to the Team, Program, and Portfolio Levels.

The concepts behind the Big Picture drew from the knowledge pools of Lean, Kanban, Scrum, and Extreme Programming (XP), as well as Don Reinertsen's *The Principles of Product Development Flow*. The distillation of these concepts into a single framework was applied in places like IBM, Discount Tire, John Deere, and Nokia with inspiring results.

Today, SAFe® is in its fourth iteration and has been adopted by 70 percent of the Fortune 100.

In its most simplistic form, SAFe® provides a framework for managing multiple business-focused streams of work within an enterprise. A kind of backlog of backlogs. It defines these within the context of portfolios of epics, or major initiatives. An epic might be a new product that you want to launch. It might be a major technology refresh program you want to undertake. It might be a new market you want to enter. It can be anything.

---

[20] *https://www.amazon.com/Agile-Software-Requirements-Enterprise-Development/dp/0321635841*

SAFe® provides a mechanism to manage and then prioritize these major initiatives and provide a bridge into both the IT and business teams that might enable this epic to be delivered.

Underneath the portfolio (epic) level is the program level. Epics are just that, epic! Each epic is broken down into a series of features and enablers which are grouped into a program increment, which is a time-bounded period where you deliver some form of business value. This value is managed by an agile release train. Within each program increment, you have a number of scrum teams who actually deliver the work. Over, you'll see a diagram showing the high-level view of this process.

The thing that is most interesting about SAFe® is its applicability across such a broad range of initiatives you might be running as an organization. The fact that by using SAFe®, Agile can be applied to far more than just software development. Agile budgeting and planning can now be used to represent and manage the entire innovation pipeline within your organization.

As an IT organization, your responsibility becomes standing up, feeding and watering a given number of downstream agile sprint teams. These multi-disciplinary teams will span different technologies. They will have different skillsets. They will do different things. But they will be there, willing and able, to work through the constant stream of requirements delivered up and prioritized by the business. No more functional requirements. No more detailed business cases. No more friction between the business and IT. Peace, and hopefully, harmony.

This brief description doesn't begin to do justice to the intricacies, or power, of SAFe®. When you fully understand it and see it in action, you will appreciate its power and how useful it can be. For more information on SAFe®, please see *www.scaledagile.com*.

What we seek to do here is simply to signpost you towards SAFe® and to start to think about how Agile, applied at scale, can be that bridge between the business and IT. A bridge between your Business Operating Model and your IT Operating Model.

Here is the authors' forecast: The businesses that crack the implementation of Agile development and the power of public Cloud will be the businesses most likely to succeed in the next decade.

So, the most important objective for the implementation of a Digital Operating Model is to create the way for real time interactive collaboration of the business team with the technology team. It's called Agile. It's that simple.

It all starts with an idea ...

We spoke earlier about how, as a company, you need to "disrupt yourself" to maintain relevance in the marketplace, but how can this be accomplished? How can we compete with the fresh ideas of the start-ups?

Consider your advantage: The people in your company and your existing customer base that can be leveraged. Your employees and customers have a wealth of experience and knowledge that can be called upon. Within these people are gold nuggets of ideas waiting to be implemented! We just need to consider how we can effectively mine for them.

Therefore, make sure you allow a forum for these ideas to be captured. This can be achieved through probing surveys (internal or external) and an ideas portal for example. Such an ideas portal could allow for voting and alike to measure demand.

Your organization should be able to take onboard these ideas and pivot accordingly. But how do we sort the wheat from the chaff? We need to validate there is of course demand as well as value to the business.

Assessing the value of ideas allows the organization to prioritize the good ideas for further analysis and possible implementation. Such value to the business can be ascertained through a number of different prioritization frameworks such as MoSCoW (Must Have, Should Have, Could Have, Won't Have), RICE (Reach, Impact, Confidence, and Effort), WSJF (Weighted Shortest Job First) or even just HiPPO (Highest Paid Persons Opinion)!

We then transition these ideas to our backlog in the form of epics, features, user stories or even just improvements or bugs. With Agile budgeting in line with the SAFe® framework, we now also have a value stream that these ideas can be funded by alongside the previously identified backlog items.

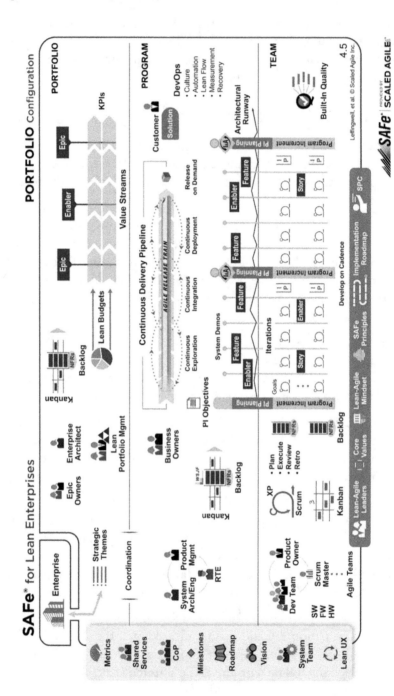

Figure 6 - SAFe® Portfolio Configuration © scaledagileframework.com

Chapter

6

The Business Questions

Take the attitude of a student, never be too big to ask questions, never know too much to learn something new.

Og Mandino (1923 - 1996), American Author

IN recent times the leadership team have been subject to increasing scrutiny of their understanding and oversight of the technology that is a foundation of the business. That does not mean to say they have to explain how the organization has embraced DevOps. It does mean they need to be ready to talk about and explain the commitment to build an organizational capability to put technology to work in this digital age – and the core of that conversation is explained in Part 1.

We have divided these questions into the same structure as the chapters within the Part 1 above. If you need some context around the questions, flick back to the chapter to which they refer to give yourself a quick reminder on the rationale of the question, or to help you best answer it.

There are no right or wrong answers. As this book suggests, consult others and seek advice from your vendors or from a business partner. This is important work.

1. **Chapter 2** – The Digital Wave
2. **Chapter 3** – The Way Ahead
3. **Chapter 4** – Digital Countdown - The Race is On
4. **Chapter 5** – Agile - small word, quick work

6.1 The Digital Wave

Have you encountered an organization lately that only deals with others by phone and post? No. We are in a digital age and it is expected of every organization that they understand what that means. We talk about that as a digital wave and it is unstoppable. The words disruption and transformation are so topical now. What is your conversation about?

In this chapter above, we discussed the environment that is driving the agenda of organizations as they consider:

- The Business Model and its relevance in a digital age
- Disruption – what disruption?
- Creating Value – the output of transformation
- The Business Operating Model (BOM)
- The extraction of value from data

We will now give you some questions to ask yourself and others about these topics.

☒	Question	Why this matters
☐	6.1.1 Has your industry experienced disruption from new entry technology-based alternatives?	If you are operating in a sector that is already used to disruptive change (like Retail or Media) then you are already attuned to understanding the impact of change. If your sector has long-standing tradition and/or is regulated (e.g. Finance, Accounting and Legal) then there are good reasons why it hasn't had a major impact so far. That does not mean to say major changes are not coming. For example, Retail Banking is now being disrupted by challenger banks. Developments such as blockchain, robotic process automation, machine learning and artificial intelligence are forecast to turn these services sectors on their heads. Is that in 1 year, 5 years or 10 years? That is the bet.
☐	6.1.2 Is the Board on-board with Cloud?	The availability of on-demand "pay as you go" computing services means that the business teams' ideas can be quickly tested and deployed into production. The application of Agile, Cloud and DevOps are fast becoming established structural pillars in organizations that are innovative in their use of technology. The speed with which your organization can test and deploy new ideas is the goal of achieving agility. The Board may not understand the mechanics of achieving agility yet must understand its importance. Is that the case?

☒	Question	Why this matters
☐	6.1.3 How do you characterize the current state of adoption of Cloud by your competitors? For that matter how do you think they characterize you?	Before you start to worry if your competitors are about to steal your lunch, ask what you know about your (and their) state of readiness with Cloud computing and the associated advanced implementation toolsets?

Microsoft [21] suggest three states of readiness:

Foundational: Organizations with little to no Cloud experience are still envisioning Cloud and require end-to-end guidance for Cloud adoption.

Intermediate: Organizations with foundational Cloud experience. Have an understanding of Cloud technologies and are either evaluating or have migrated non-priority workloads to the Cloud.

Advanced: Organizations with advanced Cloud experience are in the process of Cloud adoption and want to optimize workloads on the Cloud.

When did you last check the available sources of information that show the uptake of Cloud computing in your sector?

Are you a leader or follower? Should you be investing in being a leader?

Note: Cloud readiness and Cloud maturity (see Part 2, Chapter 8) are different.

---

[21] Extract from Adopting the Cloud Operating Model

[X]	Question	Why this matters
☐	6.1.4 How dependent is the delivery of your Business Model on IT?	Take a guess. Ask others and compare. What does that tell you? The business model has many moving parts and a supply chain and value chain. It likely relies heavily on fast and efficient collaboration and that comes with complexity. If your business process is heavily dependent on IT for ordering, inventory management, delivery and the like, then you are more likely to be able to benefit from (or suffer from) IT (Cloud) related disruption. Are you actively exploring how your customers want to be served and delivering the optimum customer experience, because if you are not then you may lose out to others that are attentive to the search for smarter (including cheaper) ways to do that.
☐	6.1.5 When did you last review how the partnership works between the business and the IT team or your IT partners?	If your organizational structure does not support a bidirectional exchange of ideas with the IT team (and suppliers and independent advisors), then you might be missing out on a raft of innovation opportunities. Many of the new functions offered by public Cloud computing platforms are complex and understanding the potential they have within your organization can only be done as an open collaborative on-going discussion. We have an idea and want to do this? Why? It makes it easier for us to serve our customers. What do you want to change about how you serve them today? If the answer is technology enabled, then the IT team/partner needs to be right in the mix to advise what is available.

☒	Question	Why this matters
☐	6.1.6 When did you last review your competitive position?	IT is the enabler and deliverer of an increasingly digital world. Cloud computing makes everything digital more accessible to organizations of all sizes. What that means is your competitors who may not have the resources you have, because they do not have the capital, can now use Cloud to compete on a level playing field. That is a game changer. Are you in this new game? Are you seeing more new entrants in your sector? Are they having an impact?
☐	6.1.7 Do you see (and treat) IT as both a threat and a potential competitive advantage?	IT now needs to be tightly linked to everything from strategy to delivery, and Board level representation is now mandatory. If your organization still treats IT as a supply and demand relationship, then you may be missing out on the know-how of your IT team. It is most likely that disruption will come at you from a technology-based platform – are you protecting that flank?
☐	6.1.8 Have you considered how you might optimize your customers' 'shop' and 'convenience' experiences using technology?	If you take heed of where disruption in many sectors has occurred, it is in these two areas. 1. how clients search and shop for a product or service. 2. how conveniently (and sometimes how quickly) that is delivered. Delivering a value proposition based on time and convenience differentiation can justify a price differential. Technology has served the pursuit of differentiated value propositions and will continue to be the primary vehicle for doing so. Do not overlook equipping employees with technology where they support the delivery of your value proposition.

☒	Question	Why this matters
☐	6.1.9 Do you have a culture to encourage innovation?	If you believe innovative ideas can come from anyone then the culture needs to be able to elevate those ideas to the appropriate discussion forums. Some believe innovation should be centered within a Lab format with a budget and start-up culture. You need to enable and actively promote the propagation of ideas, trial and error, and reward the effort (rather than the result) no matter which model you adopt. Don't expect overnight results – this process takes time particularly in large organizations. The result may in the end be the one great idea that supercharges the organization.
☐	6.1.10 Do you collect data, or do you distil it into much its more valuable cousin, information?	Organizations collect an ever-expanding universe of data – with an associated cost to retain and protect. The real value of data is revealed by the science of data analytics (aka Business Intelligence). Data is data and what organizations strive for is value from that data and extraction of that value is a function of people and technology. There is no shortage of technology. A more fundamental question is: are you training people with the skills required to analyze information?

[X]	Question	Why this matters
☐	6.1.11 Does your technology team understand what your business does, and what makes it different to its competitors?	If not, then there is work to do. You can't expect the IT team to contribute to the innovation agenda if they don't 'get' the basics of the why, what and how of the organization's existence. The history of IT has pigeonholed technologists (they just do tech, don't they?). Not anymore, they are key to unlocking the potential of technology for transformation of the 'always done it this way' and delivering 'new ways' to innovate (overused word but forget it at your peril).
☐	6.1.12 Are you set up to think and act like a challenger or more steady as she goes?	Taking a bet to disrupt a business model (to be a challenger) is a major decision point for most organizations. If you don't prepare for it, history informs someone else will. If you want to be a challenger what do your answers to the questions before say about your propensity to be a challenger?
☐	6.1.13 Which of the myths exposed in Chapter 2 did you most readily agree with?	What does that tell you about your organization's current stance? Have you discussed this with others in the organization and is there a consensus? If there is then you may be susceptible to 'group-think' so, consider inviting independent external validation of your stance.
☐	6.1.14 How would you characterize your capability to process data into information?	This is one test of your organization's agility, the capability to react to an event with the analysis of data to reveal insights to support decision-making. Can you think of an example where decisions were made on a hunch when you really wanted more information? In a world where governance is becoming ever more important, what capability needs to exist to support governance with high quality information?

[X]	Question	Why this matters
☐	6.1.15 When did you last perform a skills audit of your IT team?	The capability of your IT team to support the organization's digital journey is make or break. What skills gaps does this book expose?
☐	6.1.16 Do you have a committed budget for the Continuing Professional Development (CPD) of your IT team?	Big changes are occurring with the availability of Cloud services and your team need to be ready and equipped to face off the challengers to your business model as many of them are born in the Cloud and Cloud savvy. The rate of innovation necessitates on-going CPD and of course there are partners as a source of knowledge.
☐	6.1.17 Is your IT team competent to present the organization's value proposition?	In the past it may not have mattered. Today with IT at the core of the organization's value proposition it is vital. Those that set out with disruptive ideas understand how technology underpins the value proposition and that is becoming a key attribute of an organization equipping itself in this digital age.
☐	6.1.18 Do you have an Innovation Lab?	You may ask; why do we need one? If you accept that your current business model may be under threat of disruption, then where is the source of new ideas that will spark your reinvention? This potential for disruption is perpetual so how is that addressed?
☐	6.1.19 What skills are needed for your core 'tech' competency?	A skills audit reveals your current skills base. Are they skewed to support existing IT assets? What are the skills you consider to be core 'tech' competencies for the next five years? This book will help you answer this question.

☒	Question	Why this matters
☐	6.1.20 What is the organization's appetite to use Cloud services?	The own and operate model for IT is a comfortable place albeit with an overhead. There is a gravitation to the Cloud (evidence its meteoric growth) and that can challenge that comfortable place. Are you being left behind? If the future is a growing reliance on Cloud services what are the implications for you?

6.2 The Way Ahead

What is the capacity of your organization to absorb change?

What is driving that change?

It seems that technology is at the core of change and the rate of innovation is hard to keep up with. Still you don't want to get left behind so you need a plan and that is bigger than the selection of technology.

In this chapter above, we discussed the drivers of change and some of the big implications that weigh on the leadership team as they consider their responsibility to stakeholders.

Some questions follow to spark the conversation to shape the way ahead.

☒	Question	Why this matters
☐	6.2.1 How does your organization think and talk about digital transformation?	Is this a live conversation or background noise? Who is taking the lead; the business team, IT team, or have you (as this book suggests) joined up? For some, digital transformation has become a "catch-all" budget winner for all of the pre-existing change that was already occurring. Others have decided on implementing one initiative, e.g. let's create a mobile App for our clients. In reality, digital transformation should be on-going, focused on reinventing parts of the business model and the way they are delivered - incremental and agile (vs. monolithic and large scale).
☐	6.2.2 Does the IT function have a seat at the top table?	Does the Board recognize the significance of the Digital Operating Model? If most organizations are becoming (in part at least) highly specialized 'digital' organizations, then surely it makes sense to have digital experience represented at board level. Go one better and appoint Non-Executive Directors with digital experience to challenge the status quo.
☐	6.2.3 Are you looking for clues in your data to inform the business about what actions to take?	A digital business uses its data as an asset and mines it to reveal hidden nuggets of information. There are Business Intelligence tools now to automate processing of data and visualize as information for human consumption. Yet it still needs to be eyeballed by someone to interpret the data generated. Machine and human combined. It is fast becoming mainstream for an organization to develop this competency. Are you?

☒	Question	Why this matters
☐	6.2.4 Do you access the experience of your staff?	Technology is pervasive in our lives and for some it is a hobby or even an obsession. Younger generations change their preferred mode of communication with increasing frequency, and they seem to intuitively know which application to use (this week) for which purpose. They suppress their inner pride and pass this knowledge (with much rolling of eyes) to their older friends and relatives. This latent skill set of young people in your employee base is valuable to the organization. Do you provide a way for your people to share ideas with an incentive to do so? And do you listen when they do? Perhaps the new young hire in dispatch has some great ideas – will they remain just ideas or maybe deliver a quantum improvement in the work of the dispatch team?
☐	6.2.5 Go big or small?	The word transformation conjures up big change but that is not the only way. One approach is to begin a process of micro-segmentation. Look at the Line of Business (LoB) application suite, what can you reimagine and make Cloud native on a 'as you go basis'. Enhancing a LoB application with new functionality? Is there a Cloud service as an alternative? Another is to look outside the organization and to learn what others are doing and consider if that is an option. To quote Deloitte [22] from their report Courage under fire: Embracing disruption; 'digital should be defined based on business needs'.

[22] https://www2.deloitte.com/global/en/pages/risk/articles/directors-alert-courage-under-fire.html

☒	Question	Why this matters
☐	6.2.6 Is IT viewed as Cost Centre or a Profit Centre?	If the IT function reports into the CFO, then a cost centered IT mindset is most likely. Splitting off a chunk of IT (and its budget) and aligning it with the line of business management functions will likely yield results that would not otherwise be available. The business needs to be able to engage directly with IT. In turn, IT need to be able to understand the needs of and feedback directly to the business leads. Breaking individuals out of IT and spreading them throughout the business teams is not new. Some like the more radical approach of devolving some IT functions completely to the business and deploying a well-coordinated matrix management approach to deliver on agility.
☐	6.2.7 Is change feared?	Who likes change? We've been here before when Cloud was the hot topic of conversation for the IT team and thoughts turned to; "So, what does this mean for my future?" Putting the IT team alongside the business team breaks down this fear as the IT team is integral to the success of the business team. Maybe for once they also share in the rewards? No conflict of interest arises and what needs to get done, gets done.

☒	Question	Why this matters
☐	6.2.8 How do you set the stage for the future you are envisioning?	'I hate unsolicited spam emails!' is a common complaint from workers at all levels, and some are just downright inappropriate and unwelcome. However, this never-ending stream of approaches and offers is still one of the best methods of easy to access competitive intelligence, new ideas and market data. Attitude to spam and making time to attend educational events is an interesting cultural litmus test. Most employees are simply too busy to conduct untargeted, open-ended outbound market research. Should you provide filtered "commuting time" reading from sources that are curated under the direction of the leadership team?
☐	6.2.9 Is digital on the agenda of every board meeting.	The financial crisis of 2007-8 revealed no organization is too big to fail. More recently the failure of organizations is often linked to the fact their business model did not evolve with changes in the external environment in which they operated. In an increasingly technology driven world the Board is dealing with a new phenomenon. Taking ownership of the digital strategy is becoming a new benchmark of the board's competency. Too busy? Then consider creating a committee tasked to advise the board on all matters related to the use of digital.

☒	Question	Why this matters
☐	6.2.10 Who owns the Digital Operating Model?	There is no right answer to this question. The Digital Operating Model upon its implementation becomes an organizational practice – "It's the new way we do things around here". Supporting it with a Cloud Adoption Framework will help to coordinate and organize the organization's resources. Implementation - look at how other practices were embedded in the organization to see what worked best.
☐	6.2.11 What capacity and competencies do you think you need to develop software?	In this book we advocate keeping a core 'tech' team that is interfaced to the business teams and has competency to translate the needs of the business and deliver a solution. Decisions will need to be made as to what software is developed in-house and what is served up in the Cloud. How many people and what competencies are needed are then framed under the Digital Operating Model and the Cloud Adoption Framework. When all is said and done, some central coordination is necessary for reporting on cost control and governance.

☒	Question	Why this matters
☐	6.2.12 Who has the responsibility to stay abreast of what public Cloud services can do to enhance your competitive edge?	This role is understanding the art of the possible and fits with the experimentation that is so easy to enable in the Cloud. Ideas can flow from the business teams to IT or vice-versa and someone has to be a translator and up to-date with what is available from public Cloud services. Public Cloud vendors are releasing new 'above the IaaS line' functionality almost every day. These features and functions might just present exactly the functionality you are looking for, so you don't have to build it. Keeping abreast of these developments is important to driving tech-led innovation. Who does this? Psst, it's a full-time job.
☐	6.2.13 As the balance of expenditure on Cloud services versus legacy systems changes what is the impact on the business case?	There is always competition for expenditure and a hurdle metric for deciding which projects get the go ahead. With legacy systems you had to justify capital expenditure and the recurring cost of support and maintenance over the lifetime of the project. With public Cloud it is on/off and you only pay for what you use. However, legacy code still carries costs. As a quip: If it's not paying off, then turn it off!

☒	Question	Why this matters
☐	6.2.14 Have you evaluated if a 'Cloud first' strategy right for you?	Cloud First is interpreted as 'the solution to a requirement must first be met by Cloud, and only if that is not viable then consider an alternative'. SaaS, PaaS, IaaS in that order. FaaS glues it all together. This principle is applied and tested against what is most important to the organization, for example: Scalability, Resilience, Agility, Cost, Innovation and Compliance to name a few. Cloud is not the right answer for some workloads. Large enterprises support an IT legacy and the decision as to whether or not you should 'lift and shift' this legacy into the Cloud is complex and certainly non-trivial.
☐	6.2.15 Do you have (or are you) an internal Cloud evangelist (supported by a senior business Cloud champion)?	It is not always the case that everyone will be on-side for the Cloud. Having an evangelist ensures that there is a balance of protagonist and antagonist. In the culture of most large enterprises where change can be glacial by nature, find an energized charismatic evangelist with business acumen, give them the support they need and let them do their thing.
☐	6.2.16 Have you identified your 'Lighthouse Project?	The term lighthouse project refers to a model project that aims, besides its original purpose, to have a signal effect for numerous follow-up projects as they look towards it for inspiration and guidance. Ideally choose something that everyone can benefit from (e.g. payslips online?). In addition to success, a great notoriety is intended (Thanks Wikipedia).

☒	Question	Why this matters
☐	6.2.17 Do you understand the concept of 'above the IaaS line' benefits of Public Cloud?	Many today still completely miss the real value of public Cloud. When the National Institute of Standards and Technology first defined Cloud in 2012 many disagreed with some elements of the definition (e.g. must include "orchestration") because they weren't at that time widely available! An adjusted temporary working definition (read "IaaS") was used for much of the ensuing period. The legacy of the confusion means that today many still see Cloud and IaaS as synonyms. They are not. The real value of public Cloud in the future will come from the exploitation of the PAYG [23] availability of Software, Platforms and Functions as a Service (see Chapter 4).
☐	6.2.18 Are you in a position to exploit these 'above the IaaS line' benefits?	The Cloud may deliver bottom line savings and the point here is to ask if you are just switching on Cloud or also mobilizing people to work differently. To truly be Cloud native your organization needs eventually to move away from concepts such as servers and monolithic application suites. The very essence of the server-based model for how we deployed applications in the past creates implicit scaling restrictions. Ideas such as microservices, and the micro-segmentation of applications has been shaping the future of third-party Cloud native application development for a while now. If you have not expanded the edges of your in-house IT environment (and thinking) into the public Cloud, then accessing, integrating and using these tools to exploit your data and work differently just isn't viable.

---

[23] Pay-As-You-Go

☒	Question	Why this matters
☐	6.2.19 Have you begun to explore mechanisms for enabling (whilst still governing) the use of public Cloud?	The potential for runaway cost is one common objection inhibiting adoption of Cloud. An important aspect of your production Cloud environment is ensuring that cost transparency and management reporting is inbuilt. To satisfy this demand there has been an explosion in the availability of tools and specialized service providers – use them.
☐	6.2.20 Do you engage independent market analysts?	If you only listen to vendors, you get a vendor specific view. While there may be legacy compatibility issues and loyalty of a long-standing relationship to consider, the choices available in the Cloud are vast. Specialized independent (and ideally sector specific) market analysts can offer new perspectives. If you take a moment to think about the diversity between early adopters and technology laggards in the Cloud world it is more pronounced than in any preceding iteration of IT change. The Cloud savvy have accelerated away from the pack. Accordingly, trying to catch up with the leaders using only your own resources is unlikely to work. Skilled resources in this space are very sought after – so get some help.
☐	6.2.21 Do you have your own #challengers platform?	The #challenger is your internal secret weapon. Young, analytical, 'tapped in', socially active and aspirational. By providing a platform for your #challengers to bring forward ideas, and rewarding them for doing so, is one way to keep a #challenger mentality alive and attract more to your firm.

6.3 The Race is On

Ten years ago, few would have described technology as a race, and it was only necessary to watch what your peers were doing and tune in to what your preferred vendors were saying. Today that has that all changed. With the economics of the Cloud and a dazzling array of innovation being churned out fast, that is accessible not only to your peers but also those plotting to disrupt your business. If that feels uncomfortable – good, because if it did not then you would be complacent and that is not where you want to be.

In the past a CEO would not usually be asked a question about technology. If they duck the question today alarm bells start ringing. If you read the news, then you will know the CEO carries the can for technology – success and failure. Clearly, they are not expected to deliver a sermon on Agile (Chapter 5). Rather they are expected to articulate the big picture of how the organization will respond to the opportunities of this new era of technology on tap. If they choose to frame that with the aid of this book as their Digital Operating Model, then they now have the way to do that.

Some questions follow, use them to go layers deeper in getting to a known position that everyone on the leadership team is comfortable with.

☒	Question	Why this matters
☐	6.3.1 Do you wait for innovation to come knocking on your door?	Some organizations appoint a person or small team to go hunting for and be the receptor (to suppliers) for absorbing innovation. A detailed understanding of the business is needed to recognize opportunities to put new ways of working to use enabled by technological innovation. If digital is at the heart of every business, then you will want that to be the very best it can be. Do you expect innovation to find you, or you to find it?
☐	6.3.2 Are you measuring the right things, or are you just focused on measuring things right?	Sometimes we can't see the wood for the trees, and we follow old patterns because that's what we do. Data is the new science and art of business in the digital age. It is a major focus for the tech industry that develops software to analyze data and for customers hungry to analyze data. Don't recognize this? Perhaps you do not have the expertise in-house - so then look outside for assistance.
☐	6.3.3 Are you in the race?	It may or may not matter? Every organization will have some interest in how they stack up against others. Are you investing in technology or investing in building a capability to use technology? They are not the same. Few organizations would say they do not have enough technology, rather it is the case it is a heavy load to carry. The Digital Operating Model described in this book is about building a capability to support the 'business, people and technology' [24] for this digital age.

---

[24] As reported in Microsoft document 'Adopting the Microsoft Cloud Operating Model'

☒	Question	Why this matters
☐	6.3.4 When was the last time the board was presented an opportunity and risk assessment of all data held by the organization?	Data is a strategic resource, an asset and also a liability. We are witnessing increasing regulation around data privacy and ultimately the board is accountable. The board's task is growing in complexity as it weighs opportunity and risk associated with data. How do we take advantage of AI while complying with our legal obligations to data privacy? Ethical questions arise that need careful consideration and communication for uniformity of implementation. The new smarts are building an organizational culture that sees customers' data as an asset for building trust and not blindly applying technology to analyze the data. Do that well and it is a win-win.
☐	6.3.5 Are your people still tied to the office?	Productivity is easy to define, often hard to measure and an endless pursuit. The race for a work/life balance, reducing the waste (and environmental impact) and cost of commuting time and convenience of mobile working is wrapped up in the productivity sum. The Cloud has been an enabler of mobile working. Have you explored all the opportunities available in the Cloud in your pursuit of productivity?

☒	Question	Why this matters
☐	6.3.6 Are your business processes customer and employee friendly?	In an age where convenience is highly valued and aided by technology then throw in some friendly. Making friendly can be as straightforward as making something simple and reducing the work. "None of us is as smart as all of us" [25]. If you are looking for innovation to apply to your processes then the Cloud is the place to look, that is where smart people (developers) make available innovation.
☐	6.3.7 Do you say: "so what to transformation?"	If it ain't broke, don't fix it. True enough yet in a fast-paced world the new skill is anticipating what's coming down the road that will knock you down. It is then a question of how quickly you can react to new situations be they threat or opportunity. In this book we promote the Cloud as the foundation for delivering agility and building a competent organizational practice around a Cloud Adoption Framework gives you that capability to respond quickly. The bedfellow of anticipation is preparedness. You are smart, you work out the rest.

---

[25] Quote attributed to Kenneth H Blanchard

☒	Question	Why this matters
☐	6.3.8 Have you done your homework?	Right now, there is frenzy of new technology matched by a frenzy of ideas as to how to put that to work. The oil in that engine is data and a lot of that data was obtained under consent. In some cases, you are a custodian (Data Controller and/or Data Processor) and not the owner of that data. Before you throw data at new technology e.g. Artificial Intelligence, check your consent allows that and meets your legal obligations, consult your Data Protection Officer. You are familiar with the responsibilities of a Data Protection Officer, Data Controller and Data Processor? If not, you have homework.
☐	6.3.9 Have you evaluated the opportunity and threat of AI?	Whether you are a leader or follower it is valuable to have a position on technologies that have the potential to transform work. AI is in this category. How would you classify your current position? No position, under review, quantified, applied? AI has the potential to replace human work and that has many implications to include how it may impact your HR planning.

☒	Question	Why this matters
☐	6.3.10 Have you evaluated the opportunity of Big Data?	The recent European Union General Data Protection Regulation (GDPR) has put data, and particularly Personal Identifiable Information (PII), in sharp focus. Before you plough ahead with Big Data check those involved understand the seven principles [26] of GDPR and engage a Data Protection Officer in case of any doubt. If your tech team is not aware of these principles (and many will not be) then they could land the organization under risk of investigation by a Regulator with potential for significant financial and reputational harm. Data privacy is not harmonized around the world so education (of what is permitted/lawful) must accompany the evaluation of Big Data.
☐	6.3.11 Do you have a position on the impact of Robotics and Process Automation (RPA) in your sector?	The promise of RPA is hotly contested with great differences of opinion about its impact and in particular the displacement of jobs. If you are an employer, then you have a social responsibility to take that into consideration. Conversely, RPA could be used by competitors to undermine your business model and so it is wise to be alert to this threat. Are there jobs that you have difficulty filling or retaining staff? Is that a safe place to expose RPA? Have you considered the use of RPA to release dependency on offshore processing? Big decisions ahead.

---

[26] *https://ico.org.uk/for-organisations/guide-to-the-general-data-protection-regulation-gdpr/principles/*

☒	Question	Why this matters
☐	6.3.12 Do you have a vision for your business in a digital age?	If you look back 5 and 10 years what has been the impact of technology on the work of the organization? Probably you will identify that technology has had a big impact and more recently the Cloud will have driven that agenda. So, in your vision what are digital capabilities that your organization must excel at and why are they mission critical? [27]

---

[27] A **mission critical** factor of a *system* is any factor (component, equipment, personnel, process, procedure, software, etc.) that is essential to business operation or to an organization. Failure or disruption of **mission critical** factors will result in serious impact on *business operations* or upon an organization, and even can cause social turmoil and catastrophes. Source: Wikipedia

6.4 Agile – Small Word Big Work

If you want to be that organization that innovates and delivers a true digital experience for your customers and employees, you need to become more of a software company.

As this book set out to explain, the Digital Operating Model is where people and technology huddle together to put that into effect. How?

Agile is well established in the software engineering space, but increasingly is moving into every aspect of service creation across the business and IT. Now we turn your attention to questions that you will want to discuss with colleagues.

Agile raises questions: Do we pass? Can we take that chance? Are we ready for Agile? If not, what do we need to do to be ready?

☒	Question	Why this matters
☐	6.4.1 Do you employ software developers and data analysts?	If you do employ software developers, then don't stop there. They should be given rein to focus some of their time working closely with the business teams. When they truly understand the needs of the business team, they are better equipped to deliver a solution. Different? Better? Good idea? You won't know until you put it into practice.
☐	6.4.2 Have you invested in Agile training – and not just within the IT team?	If the business and IT are to begin to engage in iterative ongoing Agile development and innovation, then a good starting point is to make sure everyone understands the big picture and reasoning behind such an approach. They also need to learn the language. How many of your business leaders know what a "sprint" is? Chapter 5 was written for this very purpose.
☐	6.4.3 Do you have an experimentation budget?	NASA and "Big Pharma" don't get it right first time every time. They accept the limitations of and learning from investment in experimentation. The IT and Business Team staff need to have some flexibility to try (and fail fast) at new ideas, and to do so they need a "slush fund" with which to experiment. How else will you sow the seeds of innovation?
☐	6.4.4 Do you measure the average time it takes for your organization to move from idea to delivery?	Such a measurement will often reveal a surprisingly slow (glacial even) innovation cycle. You may think you're reacting quickly, but if you take all of the steps in the process into account you may be unpleasantly surprised. The issue most commonly cited as an obstacle to adopting Agile is culture. Who will take the lead?

☒	Question	Why this matters
☐	6.4.5 Do you constantly test your understanding of what matters to your customers?	Customer satisfaction surveys are omnipotent, yet customers can be fickle. If your surveys show a change in how your customers perceive your products/services, how quickly can you react? In this digital age with instant and continuous drip feed of feedback it sets the challenge to respond. Even if you think you have tuned your customer experience to be the best it can possibly be, you should never stop teasing and testing your marketplace. The adoption of a radical idea that changes an entire sector can often simply be a factor of target market maturity or timing. You should begin to adjust your mindset to be as happy with a failed result as with a successful one. Failure can teach you as much as a success. Take a look at your email and voice-based call center to service younger people...they don't like to use either!
☐	6.4.6 Have you enabled cross-infection of enthusiasm?	Rather than being mandated top down, Agile is often best embraced by an organization through the process of cross-infection of enthusiasm. Pick a high profile, low risk project – such as that time reporting system that everyone loathes – and use a process of iterative feedback and improvement involving everyone to make it sing. Use staff voting on ideas to drive the outcome. This will allow everyone to see and participate in a successful example of Agile at work and let them understand how it can benefit their customers' experiences too. They will be lining up to drive their own project next.

☒	Question	Why this matters
☐	6.4.7 What is your mechanism to budget for and deliver new services?	When you're looking to do something new like launching a new client service, the business you will typically look to IT to design, quote and deliver the project. Individual projects and the budgeting associated with this can cause excessive delays and require detailed functional specifications which can change rapidly in this fast-paced digital world. You need to consider alternative more flexible mechanisms for interfacing with (and budgeting for) IT enablement.
☐	6.4.8 Have you considered having an always-on innovation team?	One way to avoid excessive governance and overhead on innovation is to establish teams of digital specialists whose sole job is to work through a backlog of innovation as imagined by the business and your clients. There is a fixed, budgeted cost for this team per month and its efficiency can be measured via the velocity of new capabilities (or problem fixes) they are delivering.
☐	6.4.9 How would we manage and measure innovation teams?	One of the advantages of having projects and budgets is to help track the success of these projects and avoid "scope creep". Success here is, however, often measured in the number of reports and artefacts created. But isn't "scope creep" really just a result of people trying to get what they actually want? Moving to a more Agile model of innovation management can have significant advantages, such as measuring progress in terms of value delivered to the business.

☒	Question	Why this matters
☐	6.4.10 How would we report on this innovation?	Agile in its raw form is good at getting things done, but poor on reporting what has and has not been done. "We'll keep going and let you know when we're done" isn't very helpful. Frameworks such as SAFe® and Microsoft's Cloud Adoption Framework can provide the required structure, business alignment and reporting that traditional project management methodologies can't really deliver in an agile world.

Part 2 Technical

Thinking of…

Building a Digital Operating Model with the Microsoft Cloud Adoption Framework for Azure?

Ask the Smart Questions

'What the technical team need to know'

Chapter 7

A New Operating Model

The definition of insanity is doing the same things over and over again expecting a different result

Falsely attributed to Albert Einstein (1879 - 1954), Theoretical Physicist

Why do we need a new operating model?

IN recent years, IT has been viewed through a lens of cost reduction. A successful CIO or CTO has been one who tamed the flow of cash exiting an IT department's shrinking budget. They would attempt to tune an already well-oiled machine to extract additional value and productivity.

Processes were brought in to streamline and control every IT operation.

Information Technology Infrastructure Library (ITIL) emerged as the dominant viewpoint of an efficient IT operation. ITIL included Service Design, Service Transition and Service Operation. These were applied to Availability, Configuration, Testing, Release, Knowledge, Change, Event, Incident and many others. It became, and is still viewed now, as the epitome of what good looks like.

As we read in Part 1 there are two competing forces in any business or IT operating model: agility and control. This is so whatever the shape or size of the organization. The business operating model craves agility whereas the IT operating model strives to deliver control.

The trend of the last two decades has been toward outsourcing, and this has exacerbated the traditional divide. The business yearns for new capabilities, services and business models, while its IT partner looks to maximize profitability by resisting change and increasing control. The basis of outsourcing is that an outsourcer can deliver an IT service much more cheaply than an internal team. That is because it can offer specialization and economies of scale. But it also requires a slick and controlled operating model. Such a model penalizes (through change control) doing anything differently from the way it is done today.

Change control is frustrating for a business having a traditional IT operating model: 'Why are we being penalized for wanting to do something better than the way we do it today? Especially if our proposed change increases customer satisfaction and delivers new services?' Often for the business 'changing something means they have found a better way of doing something or need IT to deliver services in a different way.'

The IT provider complains that the business just doesn't get it. Change is hard. Change is difficult. Change is risky. Change is dangerous. Change is something to shy away from and discourage.

In this book we challenge these preconceptions. We also challenge the view held in pretty much every organization on the planet that change is a necessary evil.

We propose a new model. We want to construct a new relationship between business and IT. This will be a new grand bargain where IT lives at the center of an organization's business operating model. IT will sit at the top table in determining strategy. IT will feel empowered and be valued in the drive to differentiate the organization's marketplace.

To do this though, we the IT department need to behave differently. We need to be equal partners rather than just service providers. We must understand the context of the requests we receive. We should become more proactive in making recommendations, suggestions and proposing new models. We must be more deeply engrained in the business operating model.

At the same time, the business also must behave differently. It needs to stop thinking of IT as a support function, detached from the important work of actually running the business. IT should not be put in a box – a service to be provided as cheaply and efficiently as possible. It should definitely not be viewed as a nuisance getting in the way of making more money. The business should think of IT as a strategic advantage, able to bring about digital differentiation within an increasingly cut-throat market.

When the entire organization decides to give customers and employees the best experience, it develops a new attitude toward change. For both actors, change becomes something to embrace and to invest in. It becomes something desirable rather than something to shy away from or discourage.

Once this decision is made, the question becomes one of "how" to move forward. This is where the Microsoft Cloud Adoption Framework for Azure comes into play.

The changing roles of CIO, CTO and CDO

The CIO role has changed over the years. This has been in response to different requirements for the management of computing systems and data. In particular, the Chief INFORMATION Officer was responsible for all of the organization's data and was its chief data custodian. But that didn't last. As we approached the Y2K years, the role of the CIO concentrated more on financial control and long-term planning for IT systems. In particular, the CIO was expected to forecast the computing needs of an organization three years ahead. They were expected to do this with insufficient data about how changes in the world would affect the organization's IT capability and spend.

When the Cloud PAYG (Pay-As-You-Go) model came into being, the power of the Chief Technology Officer increased. More importance was placed on making the correct choice in the short term as well as the long term. Less weight came to be placed on the cost of IT and more on how organizations could get a ROI from their IT spend. The Chief Technology Office and the CFO then teamed up, and we saw the decline of the CIO role.

In the last five years the requirements have changed again. Machine learning and AI services have become available to drive greater insight into an organization's data. These services are cheap and effective. Now, with the world of data ever changing and the growing importance of data for the organization, the role of the CIO has emerged once more. But interestingly enough, it has re-emerged in the form of the CDO (Chief Data or Digital Officer).

From an outsider's perspective, it's important to make the distinction. The CIO is still looking at Cloud from a monetary perspective. This includes the operating model that comes with data and next generation workloads. The CTO cares about the adoption of innovation and the ROI on technology adoption. An operating model that can best support this is an operating model that provides guard rails to support a safe environment in which to succeed, or fail, both culturally and technically. Finally, the CDO role is important. It is the first C Level role tasked with driving the adoption of public and in some cases multi-Cloud. This takes advantage of the power of AI from one Cloud while leaving standard workload management to another one.

How are Cloud Operating Models and the Digital Operating Model different?

In this book we refer to two operating models. The overarching model that covers both Business and IT we refer to as the Digital Operating Model. A Digital Operating Model describes how the business and IT can better interact with each other at a macro level within a given organization. The specific operating models that govern the lifecycle of a given IT service line is described as a Cloud Operating Model. A specific Cloud Operating Model (COM) has many similarities with a traditional IT operating model (ITOM). The fundamental difference concerns how change is dealt with and the high levels of automation possible with Public Cloud services. In a Digital Operating Model, IT continues to deliver everything it has delivered in the past such as stability and availability. But this continues in a world built on change – a world where everything changes all the time.

A traditional IT operating model starts from the pretense that change is difficult and dangerous. There is the fear that things often break when you change them.

But what if we could build a model where change is not dangerous – or at least is orders of magnitude less dangerous? That model is what we will try and construct in the following chapters.

Chapter

8

Strategy and Service Providers

Simplicity is the ultimate sophistication

Leonardo da Vinci (1452 - 1519), Polymath

Setting off in the right direction

THE first step on a journey to a Digital Operating Model is building a Cloud strategy. A move to the Cloud is a big deal. It's a big decision – a decision that will permeate every part of your business and impact every aspect of your existing IT operations. It can also be risky and is not something to do lightly.

Building this strategy can be involved. You will need to engage a lot of people across your business. Everyone must buy in to the decision that this is something we want to do. If they are not entirely convinced and not fully committed, we must know to what extent they are in support.

You might canvass your business to make a case for moving to the Cloud. The consensus might be negative or lukewarm. They might say that it's just too difficult: 'Our IT is too elderly. We can't move our data to the Cloud. We are so super special, and we just can't do it.'

We understand. Cloud is not right for everyone. We wish you all the best. Maybe we'll speak again in the future.

Nearly all organizations react in this sort of way to begin with. That includes the ones that have since fully embraced Cloud. But to be successful you will need to secure buy-in from the business and from the key IT stakeholders. As Friedrich Nietzsche once said,

"He who has a why to live for can bear almost any how." The same is true for businesses. Without a *why* this can be a very difficult path to strike out on. We will cover this topic in a little more detail later in this chapter when we introduce the Microsoft Cloud Adoption Framework section on "Define Strategy".

> If you want to jump straight to it and read about Strategy within the Cloud Adoption Framework for Azure, visit: *https://aka.ms/adopt/strategy*

For those still following, let's get down to business. We'll assume you want to do this and so it's not *if*, it's *how*. We'll assume you landed on something like "Cloud First". This advocates Cloud wherever possible, unless there's a really good reason for not adopting it.

Once you've got the green light, we'll need to get down to the detail. What does Cloud-first mean? How do we build a strategy around this? This book is not designed to educate the reader on the NIST definition of Cloud computing and does not get drawn into a debate about what is and what isn't really Cloud. When we talk about Cloud in this book, we are talking predominantly about public Cloud or Hyperscale Cloud. These are the providers who invented the concept, not those who rebranded their existing offerings.

Example of Guiding Principles for IT Strategy:

1 All applications and workload services currently hosted should be assessed for cloud migration.

2 A single user identity must prevail over all service consumption.

3 IT service delivery must be adhere to a service-centric model which includes lifecycle and evergreening.

4 All new services should adhere to a technology code of practice and architecture, in particular:
   a). Based on open standards: services should interoperate with little or no remediation.
   b). Cloud security principles: services must meet the security requirements for handling data and privacy.
   c). Public Cloud First.
   d). Native functionality cloud services is preferred over 3rd party tools.

5 All new services should use public cloud services in the following priority order:
   a). SaaS.
   b). PaaS.
   c). IaaS.

6 All cloud services, including IaaS, will be owned by customer but can be managed by 3rd Party service providers.

7 Simplicity and reliability of use for end users is of the highest priority.

8 Access to services must be restricted to permitted users and devices only and based on least privilege.

9 End user devices must be control by security policies and guidelines geared for a Mobility First strategy

10 Native functionality in client devices and access services is preferred over 3rd party tools.

11 Automation and predictive insights, where possible, must underpin the support, remediation and administration of the services delivered.

Figure 7 - Guiding principles for IT Strategy

A true Cloud strategy should focus on public Cloud. This will enable you to harness the innovation we spoke about in Part 1. Public Cloud is required if you really want to digitally transform your organization.

We now need to break Cloud down into the three main groups: IaaS, PaaS and SaaS. Again, this book will not dwell on the definitions of these things. We assume the reader understands these concepts at a high level. Your strategy needs to be cognizant of the differences between these service models and address each separately.

Cloud Center of Excellence

A great place to start on a journey towards building these standards and service-centric patterns is to create a Cloud Centre of Excellence.

Within a Cloud Centre of Excellence, teams come together to build the guiding principles. This team does not need to be a standing team of permanent members but should represent business and service staff. The objective of the CCoE is to strike a balance between speed and stability. It is a mechanism to move an organization from a regime of control and central responsibility to one of freedom and delegated responsibility.

Multi-Cloud

The two main building block services for your core infrastructure will be IaaS and PaaS – server hosting and application hosting. According to Gartner (*https://azure.microsoft.com/resources/gartner-iaas-magic-quadrant/*), there are not many true Cloud infrastructure providers to choose from. There are Amazon, Microsoft, Google, Alibaba, Oracle and IBM. Assuming you don't have significant operations in China and that you're not locked in either to Oracle or IBM, only three are left.

Your next decision is: Do I as a business support, one, two or all three of these providers?

What does all this mean? There is multi-Cloud and there is Hybrid Cloud. Some very large organizations may use both.

Multi-Cloud is a much-debated topic now. Some in the industry define the concept as a common technology layer hosted by multiple vendors. Others define it more as a deployment model that requires a common abstraction layer between different environments.

We will treat multi-Cloud as something that requires the management of different Cloud service providers. They will be both public and private and use different tools and services in a common way.

Suppose you decide to provide a suite of IaaS services from more than one Cloud provider. You will need to include the tooling and process so that services deployed into one Cloud meet the same configuration and governance standards as another.

Even for something as simple as a single virtual machine host, you may have to replicate effort in the management and maintenance of service blueprints. Management tooling may be required in multiple locations. Your brokering and orchestration layer must support multiple methods of addressing the Cloud provider's fabric. This applies whether the layer is highly automated or invoked on demand by staff. The fabric is mostly bespoke for each vendor. The tools required for service management also need to consider the subtleties of each vendor's Cloud service environment.

In the Microsoft Cloud Adoption Framework, the Ready phase covers this topic in the context of Azure based workloads. The Ready phase talks of Landing Zone considerations and best practices that provide guidance on how to address a series of design principles. These principles apply equally to all Cloud providers but may be solved in different ways.

There are, of course, ways to abstract this complexity. This can be done by consuming lower level services such as containers. But most heritage IT estates are a long way from being able to move more than a small portion of services to benefit from this type of technology.

There are several vendors and platforms which provide this abstraction for you, but they can be complex and expensive. They also often fail to take advantage of niche platform-specific capabilities from other vendors, such as Azure Cognitive Services.

There are good reasons for adopting multi-Cloud. But there are also bad ones.

For example, a good reason would be a scenario in which you consume services that are suitable for a certain public Cloud provider, while having other services that lend themselves to a different provider. If you are in this situation you may be forced into a multi-Cloud world by your application layer.

In this case you may find yourself consuming SAP® S4/HANA public Cloud as well as Oracle, IBM Bluemix, and Azure.

Alternatively, a poor reason for choosing a multi-Cloud approach would be the fear of vendor lock-in. The ability to move workloads between vendors to get the best price is not a good criterion.

We will argue in this book that multi-Cloud entails greater management complexity and operational risk. Unless dictated by regulatory bodies, this potentially outweighs any risk of committing to a single Cloud provider. Also, many Cloud providers make a charge for offloading data from their services. An architecture that moves vast amounts of data between Cloud providers doesn't make sense.

Instead, we encourage organizations to think about general-purpose and specialized operating models. We encourage organizations to pick one Cloud (we recommend Azure, naturally) as their primary, general-purpose Cloud. Your general-purpose Cloud should deliver end-to-end capabilities, including your control pane. It should deliver your core management and monitoring services across all Clouds. Any services which are common and non-differentiated between vendors (such as VMs) should only be supported within your primary Cloud. If you believe another Cloud provides a service which doesn't exist within or is substantially better than the one within your primary Cloud, support just this. Your specialized operating models can therefore be much simpler and more focused. You get the benefits of multi-Cloud without having to build multiple general-purpose operating models.

Hybrid Cloud.

Hybrid Cloud is an easier concept to grasp. It relates to the location of services within a management boundary.

Hybrid has been a core part of Microsoft's narrative since Windows Server 2012 R2, its first *Cloud OS*. The idea is that if you were running Hyper V and System Center across your on-premises estate and were consuming Azure public Cloud services, you were in effect within a single management plane. You were then able to shift workloads around to meet whatever business and technical circumstances you were faced with.

This conversation has matured over the years with the introduction of technologies like Azure Stack. This allows for a near seamless operating model across multiple physical hosting options: on premises, partner hosted and public Cloud.

For those who cannot afford Stack, you can still get a high level of integration out of the box between your on-premises environment, a third-party hosting provider, and Azure.

Microsoft also provides tools like Azure Backup, Azure Site Recovery and Azure Monitor. These will run both across on premises and Azure, providing a unified management plane for these operational services.

Hybrid Cloud can, therefore, achieve a location-based paradigm within a single set of management tools. If done right. If done wrong, hybrid can be a complexity masqueraded as flexibility.

We have now defined the concepts of multi- and hybrid Cloud. We can move on to a closer look at the architectural concepts that will determine which model you adopt.

Your estate

IT estates can be divided into end user services, which we describe as "Intelligent Workplace", and back office infrastructure and application services which we call "Intelligent Cloud". The strategy you adopt will be determined by the capability and direction of travel for these services across domains.

Your new end user compute services will incorporate public Cloud. This has an impact on the architecture of your back office and how you deploy applications to it.

Bimodal IT is a key aspect of the new IT world you are planning.

Bimodal IT

Gartner's describes a two-speed model of IT deliver.
(*https://www.gartner.com/it-glossary/bimodal/*). In this model heritage
IT assets exist alongside newer, more agile Cloud-native capabilities
and service lines.

Think Marathon Runner	Mode 1		Mode 2	Think Sprinter
	Reliability	Goal	Agility	
	Price for performance	Value	Revenue, brand, customer experience	
	Waterfall, V-Model, high-ceremony IID	Approach	Agile, Kanban, low-ceremony IID	
	Plan-driven, approval-based	Governance	Empirical, continuous, process-based	
	Enterprise suppliers, long-term deals	Sourcing	Small, new vendors, short-term deals	
	Good at conventional process, projects	Talent	Good at new and uncertain projects	
	IT-centric, removed from customer	Culture	Business-centric, close to customer	
	Long (months)	Cycle times	Short (days, weeks)	

Gartner.

Figure 8 – Bimodal IT© Gartner Inc

The Bimodal IT concept is important. We will elaborate later in the
book. At this stage you should understand the core differences
between two modes. The closer you get to Mode 2, the more
valuable the IT organization will be to the business.

The primary focus of the two modes is summed up in their
respective goals. The goal of Mode 1 is reliability. This means uptime and stability. This mode is geared to fight change. Its focus is
the efficiency of the IT estate.

Mode 2 by contrast is all about change. It describes change in a
positive light; change implements new ideas quickly and favors
business agility.

You will be developing an IT strategy to incorporate public Cloud
services. As you do so you need to think about how you architect
services to best take advantage of the fast pace of change in public
Cloud.

Your IT organization needs greater Cloud maturity. This is because
it will allow your services to respond quicker to the fast pace of
change in the business.

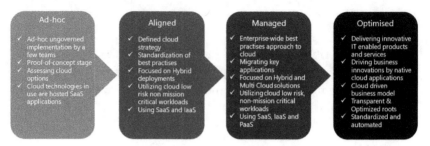

Figure 9 - Cloud Maturity Model

The ideal is that your businesses should be able to realize revenue from an idea by quickly enabling the required IT services to deliver it.

These IT services should be designed in such a way that they can be spun up and down on demand. The maintenance and health of these services should be highly automated.

You may not achieve all this at the first pass. But the closer you get to the optimized model the greater will be the benefit to you and your businesses.

One of the keys to success is to operate both modes initially. This is why it is called Bimodal IT. You can't just abandon your Mode 1 heritage workloads. The estate is running your business today and much of it will be running your business in 12 to 18 months from now.

It is also important that you begin to incorporate services architected for native public Cloud.

Many organizations begin by introducing small applications and services that supplement existing, deeply embedded COTS applications.

An example would be extracting key data from an on-premises line of business application into Azure Data Services. You could then write a mobile app to consume this data. The app might serve a single business function and might be read-only. You could create a business process to update data in the underlying application. When the data got updated, you could automatically push this update to the app and notify the user. This model allows users to see this new piece of information in near real time without you having to rebuild or re-architect the underlying legacy line of business application.

A small set of applications like this can spring up around a core LOB application. They will add huge amounts of value. There is no need to invest large amounts of effort and money in re-engineering the core application at this stage. This composite model of application development is particularly useful as you embark on your journey to the public Cloud.

In the future, major software vendors will rewrite their applications to work natively in the public Cloud. Until then you will need to support your IT in both modes.

The Microsoft Cloud Adoption Framework for Azure – Define Strategy

Having discussed some high-level considerations, let's now jump into the specifics as they relate to Microsoft's view on strategy. As you would expect, Microsoft kicks off their Cloud Adoption Framework for Azure with a stage called "Define Strategy".

> To read more about Strategy within the Cloud Adoption Framework for Azure, visit: *https://aka.ms/adopt/strategy*

In this phase, the framework speaks to a need to understand the motivations of a Cloud migration. It also advises to understand the justification and outcomes from a business perspective of any migration program and to identify a potential first workload or workloads to move.

Research has shown that organizations that understand their motivation are far more likely to undertake and complete a Cloud transformation program.

When assembling your list of potential business outcomes, the Microsoft Cloud Adoption Framework provides some categories for this discussion. It organizes this thinking into a business outcome framework that covers subjects such as fiscal, agility and performance outcomes. There is also some guidance on how to capture this information.

This step is critical as you commence your journey to a Digital Operating Model. Unifying the business and technology teams around a common strategy and set of goals is paramount.

Many Microsoft partners will have consulting engagements in this space. You will need to cover the subjects of aligning the business strategy to the IT strategy, the readiness of the environment to connect Cloud services, the relative maturity of your organization across a wide spectrum of elements, and finally the economic position pre- and post-Cloud migration.

The Cloud Adoption Framework Benchmark tool provides an excellent way to understand the current state of relationships between your business and technical teams. It also allows you to rate your relative Cloud maturity with peers in the market. Visit: *https://aka.ms/adopt/gov/assess*

It is also essential to have a business case that stacks up. Your driver might be a datacenter exit and the avoidance of a large capital expenditure at one extreme. Alternatively, you might be motivated by increasing the speed of the IT organization and reduce your "time to value". In either situation, it is important that you know what the 3–5 year likely cost profile is.

Service Provider Relationship

There is another important aspect of adopting public Cloud. There will be a change in the relationship between you and your Cloud vendor.

In the past you bought software from, say, Microsoft, Oracle, or IBM. You either ran this software yourself or paid someone else to run it for you. This is a classic ITOM model. Responsibility for the software is separate from the responsibility for delivering it.

In a Cloud world, these functions are often blurred. The creator of the software now delivers the software (or platform) to you as a service.

Occasionally in a non-Cloud world, actions of the software vendor can cause you real pain. A bad update for example. But most of the time you are responsible for and in control of your IT service.

In the present world, when something goes down, anyone, even the CEO, can come down and get grumpy with you until you fix the problem. Their presence doesn't make the situation any better, and in fact often makes it worse. But at least they have the satisfaction of feeling that they are getting involved and, in their eyes, *helping* to get the problem solved.

In the new world of Cloud, there is no room for them to come down to! No one to come and shout at! There is nothing anyone can do to *assist* in bringing the service back up. There's only one thing you can do: that is to let the users know there's a problem and that it's in hand. Then you can sit on your hands and wait. This can be incredibly disconcerting for both you and the business. Suddenly, it no longer matters who shouts loudest. Services will be brought back online, as quickly as possible, in the best technical way. If SLAs have been breached, you'll get credits back. There are no consequential losses, and no punitive damages.

Whilst this can be off-putting and indeed scary in some situations, there are nevertheless some positives. When things go down, it's stressful – very stressful. We've all been there late at night or over a weekend battling to get something back online. It's not something you'd wish on your worst enemy. It's not something you'll miss from your past.

In the Cloud world, you may not feel personally as important as you used to be. You're actually part of something much more important. You are part of a much bigger collective. You're just one of millions of users who are also getting very grumpy. There's nothing like a service that caters to millions of users for getting the attention of vendors. And so, on the very rare occasions that things do go down, they tend to come back up very quickly.

You can, of course, mitigate some of these risks with a multi-Cloud and multi-vendor approach. But you need to carefully consider the pros and cons of such an approach. The question to ask is: Is some downtime acceptable if it has significant savings in terms of cost and complexity? Do you really have to push for that 99.999 percent SLA?

This change of relationship is a profound one. It is a change from a supplier/customer relationship to a partnership relationship. As you move to the Cloud, your fate and your service provider's fate become intertwined. Their success is your success; their failure is your failure. It's a momentous change, and one you need to be fully prepared to accept. The buck no longer stops with you; it stops with them as well as you. You need to be immersed in this idea of shared responsibility.

This is a new normal approach, and one to be shared by service providers and consultancies.

Service Level Agreements

This new partnership-based relationship necessitates KPIs and other measures to govern it. The service descriptions and operating commercial agreements now become enormously important documents. They govern the gives and gets of the relationship down to the lowest level of detail. The service level agreement is the more important one. It commits providers to make available xyz service to you, a minimum of 99.9x percent of the time.

> For details of the SLAs provided by Microsoft Azure, visit:
> https://azure.microsoft.com/en-us/support/legal/sla/

Your partnership depends on this key metric. It will govern what success looks like for your provider. As a guide, 99.9 percent service corresponds to about 45 minutes of downtime a month. At 99.99 percent that figure is reduced to about 4½ minutes a month. Providing service downtime doesn't exceed those limits; all will be well.

However, it's important to dig deeper into these SLAs. Different services have different SLAs. Office 365 guarantees 99.9 percent uptime. Single instance VMs in Azure come with a 99.9 percent uptime guarantee. But this can be increased to 99.95 percent with an availability set, and even to 99.99 percent with two availability sets. Just to increase the complexity, SLAs can interact with each other. Suppose you have a load balancer with a 99.95 percent SLA in front of a VM with a 99.95 percent SLA. This is equivalent to an SLA of only 99.9 percent (99.95 percent * 99.95 percent = 99.9 percent). You depend on both and each can go down .05 percent of the time. That gives a combined downtime of 0.1 percent. It's vital to understand these compounding SLAs. At the least, you should at least understand the concept. It is highly relevant to your evaluation of what a service provider is committing to.

These are some of the issues to guide you in selecting your multi-region or multi-Cloud strategy.

Support

Support is a broad concept and an issue we will investigate in more detail in the section on service management. But for now, it needs to be pointed out that it is vitally important and should be planned for up front.

The questions to ask are: When something goes wrong, who is going to respond? How are they going to interact with the service provider? What kinds of support does your service provider offer? Are there escalated tiers of support available either to you or to other providers you partner with?

Getting the support relationship right and defining it properly are keys to the success of your new Cloud environment.

We cover many of these topics in more detail in other chapters. For the purpose of this strategy chapter there are some high-level concepts to consider.

The Microsoft Cloud Adoption Framework covers this subject matter in the "Plan" phase. The key sections here to familiarize yourself with are the section on "Initial Organization Alignment" and the section on Skills Readiness.

Firstly, there should be a single owner for your service management layer. All the responsibility for governance and service operations need to be given to someone with a holistic view of your world. This person must also understand the business. It is possible to outsource this responsibility. But there are strong arguments for keeping it in house.

The orchestration of all IT services to the business requires an impartial overseer. Service models become ever more complex. There can be multiple vendors and partner relationships. This overseer primarily represents the business and his or her job is to keep everyone honest.

Secondly, you need to own your IT strategy. Bringing in expertise from external advisors and consultants is a good thing. But the Enterprise Architecture function and the ultimate arbiter of the 1-, 3- and 5-year plans should be an internal resource. We touch a bit later on the Scaled Agile Framework (SAFe®) which has its own Portfolio function that is a good replacement for TOGAF.

This Enterprise Architect or Portfolio Lead manages the direction of travel for the organization's IT services. As such they need to be accountable to the CIO and therefore to the business itself.

The EA / office of the CTO should also be thinking of ways to open new revenue streams for the business. This will be done by monetizing data and services where possible.

Lastly, you should build a cohort of suppliers behind the scenes consisting of specialist best of breed partners. You will also need partners who can provide scale when it is needed.

Many of the Global SI community are struggling to convert to Cloud services as these services cannibalize existing revenue. However, they are excellent at providing scale services such as service desk and application support.

There are lots of new Cloud-focused MSPs that can be incorporated into your service model. They will sit between you and the services and vendor management of your chosen Cloud provider.

Chapter

9

Procurement and Financial Governance

The way to stop financial joy-riding is to arrest the chauffeur, not the automobile

Thomas Woodrow Wilson (1856 - 1924), United States President (1913 - 1921)

Building a new procurement model

T HE first step on a journey to a Digital Operating Model is to build a model to support procuring your new Cloud services.

Procurement and financial governance are completely different in a Cloud world. Instead of purchasing assets such as hardware or IP rights, we consume various kinds of services. We are buying levels of capability and offerings based on very different pricing models. To understand how to procure and govern these new Cloud services you must understand what it is you are buying. Different metrics and measures apply to each service.

Some of these models are based on a fixed price per unit or per month. Typically, that applies to SaaS services. But many components have variable pricing – PaaS and IaaS services are examples.

It's important, as you build your procurement and financial controls, to take account of variability. As a rule, it's impossible to predict how much you will be spending on your Cloud services each month. Instead, think about a model which includes pre-defined, and pre-authorized blocks of spending. Additional governance and controls can be invoked if these amounts are exceeded.

The Microsoft Cloud Adoption Framework covers a section which Microsoft refer to as "What is Cloud accounting?" in the business justification section of the Strategy phase. This section covers concepts like Showback and Chargeback and combines with a section called "Creating a financial model for Cloud transformation" to give you the tools you need to begin to unpack this topic.

> To read more about Cloud Accounting, visit:
> *https://aka.ms/adopt/strategy/cloudaccounting*

The next question is: From where are you going to procure these Cloud services? In the past you might have bought hardware and software from a reseller or distributor. In the case of Microsoft licensing, you might have bought from a Licensing Service Provider (LSP). This could have been part of an Enterprise Agreement.

These licensing vehicles and partners play less of a role in the new Cloud world. Instead, organizations such as Microsoft have overhauled their licensing programs. They have adopted a more flexible, consumption-based model.

In future you will likely purchase licenses and Cloud capacity from Cloud Solutions Providers (CSPs). They handle both licensing and professional and managed services. These partners may source these licenses and capacity directly from Microsoft (direct CSPs). Alternatively, they will get them from distributors (indirect CSPs) before selling them on to you.

One of the advantages of a move to a Cloud-based consumption model is clarity and transparency of pricing. Likewise, one of the disadvantages of a move to a Cloud-based consumption model is clarity and transparency! The price is the price which is the price. In the old world, RRPs were largely ignored as organizations cut individual deals with vendors. There were large discounts available in line with scale. The best time to buy Microsoft licensing was in June, at the end of Microsoft's financial year.

In the Cloud world there are a few discounts for the very largest customers – those who spend millions of pounds per year. But discounts and complex pricing models are no longer available to most customers. Simplicity is, in the case of Cloud, the ultimate sophistication.

Procurement pipeline

At the start of your journey into Cloud you must identify your strategic Cloud provider. After that you need a plan to bring the services on board. Typically, these onboarding services are not delivered by the Cloud provider themselves but are undertaken by specialist partners.

Many organizations choose Microsoft as their strategic partner. Since you are reading this book, presumably you are one of them. Congratulations, you made a good choice. You're comfortable that Microsoft has ticked your various boxes. You're good to go on Office 365 and/or Azure. It's time to crack on. Don't let a procurement pipeline get in the way of starting to use that right now.

There will typically be other SaaS solutions which you need to procure. You need to build a process for this procurement. The process is not dissimilar to that for identifying and procuring traditional software. You'll need to go to market with your requirements and see who comes back with what. You might want a specialist solution for the automation of business processes. Or you might want an intelligent chatbot solution.

Whichever solutions you choose, it is important that they sit within the realm of your Digital Operating Model. The questions you will ask of a SaaS vendor will be different to the ones you will have asked when procuring an on-premises solution. You need to ensure that the platform that their solution is built on will integrate with your environment. If you want to run it as a service, without your environment, it must be compatible with Azure. You need to understand how it operates and how you and the vendor will support it.

Getting this procurement right will ensure you can support requests for SaaS solutions from the business. The SaaS solutions must fit their requirements. They must also meet your availability requirements. Finally, they must be secure to your standards and work for you.

Financial Operation (FinOps)

Procuring Cloud services is difficult. This is because of the variability in the commercial models of different providers and services. To deal with this the concept of FinOps or Financial Operations has been introduced. This is a new kind of operational function within your organization responsible for procurement and billing of Cloud services.

To horribly misquote Churchill: Never in the history of IT has the power to spend so much rested in the hands of so few.

Every configuration change in Cloud has a financial consequence. These come into effect immediately a service is live and ready to use; likewise, immediately after it's shut down or resized. This is not a bad thing. Indeed, part of the benefit of public Cloud lies in your power to manage the cost and benefit of IT services. This can be done almost in real time. At the same time, these costs become more transparent to the business.

The more traffic you send to a service the more resource it can be allowed to consume.

Equally, as demand for a service goes down, they can have resources removed. This will reduce the run cost.

An unfortunate example of this can be seen in the following story. An early customer of Azure engaged a consultant to undertake an introduction to Azure workloads for their company. The consultant got to the HPC (High Performance Computing) services topic just before lunch. He kicked off the provisioning of a 50-node cluster as everyone left to eat. When they all got back 45 minutes later the environment had been provisioned. But it had burned through his free £120 MSDN of monthly Azure allowance. As a result, everything had shut down!

What does the Cloud Adoption Framework say?

In the "Operate" phase of the Microsoft Cloud Adoption Framework there is a section on "Govern". The Govern section focuses on the "Five Disciplines of Cloud Governance:" which are:

- Cost Management

- Security Baseline
- Resource Consistency
- Identity Baseline
- Deployment Acceleration

The govern section also contains a guide to "Improve the Cost Management discipline" and some tooling to aid in the creation of a governance baseline for your business. The Ready section also includes guidance on how to deliver this.

> For more information on cost management within the Cloud Adoption Framework for Azure, visit: *http://aka.ms/adopt/gov/cost*
>
> and
>
> *http://aka.ms/adopt/ready/managecost*

Operational Cost Governance

Non-production workloads illustrate how costs can be managed as part of your operations ITOM layer. These workloads rarely need to be on 24/7. They can often be off for long periods. To illustrate this concept, let's suppose the release cycle for a vendor-supported application is quarterly. You may need two weeks for testing prior to release to production. But for the rest of the time the test region for the service is idle. If this service is switched off during idle periods, you can make savings on compute costs. Over time these savings will mount up.

Workloads having variable, burstable usage patterns are another case. If the patterns are known and predictable, automated tasks can be carried out on the estate to cope with them. Nodes and clusters can be scaled both vertically and horizontally.

In retail a burst can be an order of magnitude above the normal. A stamp type model could be the solution here. This incorporates a full functional cross section of an application including presentation, application and database. In this way, even very large-scale fluctuations can be handled. You no longer need to scale your environment for peak demand. In this case it may just tick over at ten percent capacity for ten months of the year.

If scale is less predictable and fluctuates over a day, auto scaling can be considered. Auto scaling works very well in a Cloud-native architecture. This is where each component is stateless and is designed to scale horizontally.

Another case is that of a microservices architecture. When each microservice is designed in a Cloud-native way you can scale up and down according to the load on the service. This is done with set parameters within the Cloud fabric.

For heritage applications you can adopt a similar approach. But it will be slightly less elegant owing to the inherent lack of flexibility of the application architecture. A remote desktop service may have ten session hosts to provide compute power to the user community. Without the use of complex tools, you would need to deploy all ten nodes into public Cloud. However, you could shut eight of them down to save the compute costs. You could then boot these servers on demand. This would be done with the auto scaling feature. It would click in when the load of the running nodes reached a pre-defined threshold.

There are many more use cases for cost management. They share a common theme. Those that will be useful to your organization will often be unique. It all depends on your scale, your geographic reach, and so on.

Build and deploy governance

This is the second topic relating to financial governance. The cost of services should be understood and correctly allocated at build time. As services are built by project services teams, they begin to incur costs.

Cost control and TCO are rarely at the front of engineering minds in the implementation phase of a project. Why have four cores on this server when eight is clearly better? Wouldn't it be risky to deploy a server with only 16GB of RAM? The next one on the list has 56GB and would be safer.

Worse still are developers who spin up multiple nodes of whatever size feels right to test something. Then they get distracted and leave them running for weeks unused. As organizations begin this journey to Cloud at scale, the financial governance topic will quickly bubble to the top of the list of priorities.

There are many ways to address this issue. Staff need flexibility to interact with Cloud services as the requirement arises. At the same time, someone, somewhere should be making financial decisions. The structure of your public Cloud environment is relevant. Azure has a combination of subscriptions, resource groups and tagging. Careful consideration must be given to role-based access and policies. You should also consider the use of Azure Policies to assist in this space as you can use this feature to limit what staff can and can't do to the environment.

There are similarities between organizations and their use of these features. Your final position will depend on several factors. These include the size of the organization, the number of teams allowed access, your geographical reach, as well as other factors. A small team located in one place may well handle this governance at team level. Access to the management tooling could be left largely open. A larger team with broad geographic spread may well lock the management console down. The same applies to one with multiple operating companies with distributed management. It may be necessary to limit interactions by delegation to a subscription or resource group.

All this needs to be thought through before you put large workloads into public Cloud.

Right Sizing and Optimization

The final topic under the heading of financial governance is workload optimization. No matter how much modelling you do, you will be deploying workloads into Cloud using a best guess. It may be a very informed and experienced guess. You may well come close much of the time. But what you are unlikely to do is watch your workloads over time to see if you can be more efficient.

Into this space drops specialist tooling. This tooling will keep watch on your VMs and PaaS workloads. Over time a view will be built of how busy they are and the resources they are consuming. This tooling will compare the resource consumption with the SKUs available to you. It will recommend changes you can make. It will also show the cost savings these changes will attract.

To learn more about optimizing costs based on recommendations, visit: *https://docs.microsoft.com/azure/cost-management/tutorial-acm-opt-recommendations*

The more sophisticated among these tools will also allow you to apply personalized polices to the optimization algorithm. In this way, recommendations you don't want will not appear. Many of the public Cloud vendors have a version of this capability baked into the management portal. Microsoft purchased Cloudyn for this purpose. This has now been integrated directly into the Azure Portal.

There are other, third party tools in market. They may give you a more granular estimate. They may present the data in a way that is easier for you and your teams to understand. Some tools also have a rich API. They can trigger run books or customized scripts if you want to automate this activity. Many of the tools available can also look at other procurement vehicles which you may be able to take care of, such as reserved instances. These are advantageous in the case of a workload that is on all the time. If you are comfortable you know the size of the VM is correct. And provided you know it is unlikely to change over time, you can purchase a reserved instance. This will attract up to a 40 percent discount on the Pay-As-You-Go pricing. We will talk further about this concept within the capacity management section in the next chapter.

Chapter

10

Service Management

If everyone is moving forward together, then success takes care of itself

Henry Ford (1863 - 1947), Industrialist

Building a new service model

S ERVICE management is the core of your Digital Operating Model. It is the nuts and bolts of the way Cloud will be born and delivered in your organization. The service management surrounding your Cloud environment will determine its success or failure. It's where the rubber meets the road between agility and control. It's your front line between the business and IT.

Service management in a traditional IT operating model is one of the best

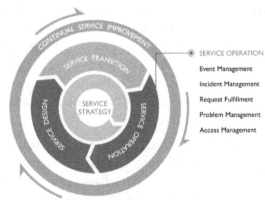

Figure 10 - ITIL Service Map

described and best designed set of standards. Information Technology Infrastructure Library (ITIL) is now in its fourth incarnation. There were major changes between v3 and v4 around management of Cloud environments. ITIL describes every aspect of IT service provision. It describes how to model and control it.

Alongside ITIL, some organizations leverage Service Integration and Management (SIAM). This divides this service provision across multiple providers. Different services can have a single interface to the business.

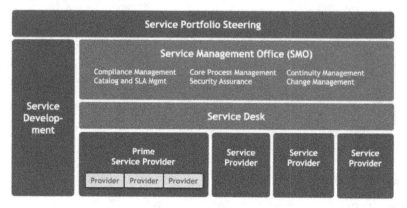

Figure 11 - Traditional SIAM Service Model © www.itforbusiness.org

These models are widely used today. They are still described as Future Operating Models (FOMs). Compared to what was available before, they are brilliant. They still offer a lot of value today. They were, however, a product of their time. And time moves on – fast...

Many organizations now feel suffocated by this siloed approach to IT delivery and accessibility. Standardization delivers a lowest common denominator approach to IT. A service catalogue should support a request for a server in the same way as a request for a laptop. A user having a problem accessing e-mail should not be treated differently from a user who is unable to run a CI deployment script.

Many Cloud service lines also cut across their parent towers. Datacenter and hosting are examples given above. How do you deal with these new service lines? How can you present them to the business with the best of what you do today? The business requires more flexibility and agility to utilize the Cloud effectively. These are some of the ideas we explore in this chapter.

A tower or a service line?

If you operate with some form of SIAM model, you'll be familiar with the concept of towers. A tower includes several service lines and interfaces to the SIAM owner. In a Cloud world, these service lines will often be described differently. They fail to sit neatly within the ontology that your current model is built upon.

With a Digital Operating Model there is a relationship between the business and the new Cloud service lines which was not there with a traditional ITOM. How do users provision services? How do they access them? How do they get support for them?

In a traditional ITOM, from a datacenter perspective, the server ruled the world. Organizations have millions of server definitions in their service catalogues. Do you want a blue one? Four CPUs or two CPUs? How many disks? How much RAM? Once you've chosen your server, you choose which environment you want it deployed into. These include Dev, UAT, Production. There will be pages and pages of options of configuration items (CIs) to deploy into. They will all be managed within your organization's ITOM.

In the new Cloud world, CIs become less important and less relevant. This is so particularly in a Cloud-native Gartner Mode 2 world. The physical and virtual manifestation of an application at any time of the day, week or month matters only from a billing and monitoring perspective. It does not matter from a support or availability perspective. Environments become ephemeral and short-lived. They can be recreated automatically on the fly. Why have just three environments for an application? You can have as many as are needed by whoever is testing which part of the system?

The key to building a successful Digital Operating Model is to free it from the confines and control of a traditional ITOM. At the same time the security and policies that your organization requires can be kept in place. The service line you're building has some similarities with a traditional tower. It still forms part of a distributed service delivery model. But there are important differences. It needs to exhibit some of the same capabilities, such as SLA delivery, for example. But it can deliver this in much improved ways – in real-time, for example.

You'll need to understand how your tower model evolves with a move to a Digital Operating Model. How will you expose the new Cloud service lines? You probably won't know the answer to that question yet. But the answer will emerge as you expose the underlying Cloud platforms. It will become clearer as you understand more about how users are consuming and demanding support on these capabilities. The general rule is the more you refine process the more agility you can deliver.

Service Portfolio Lead

To begin on your journey to a new Digital Operating Model it's useful to start to think about the notion of a service portfolio. How can you start to structure and organize the different services that IT might want to present up in a way that can be better understood? How can you create stronger links between demand and value? End User Compute doesn't mean much to a business consumer of an internal IT service. Teamwork does.

Consider whether you might be able to use a model that more closely resembles this:

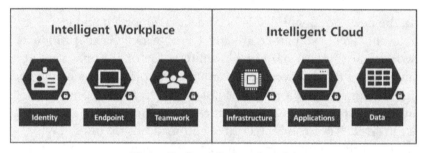

Figure 12 - Portfolio-based model

Grouping your services into this kind of portfolio-based model makes it much simpler for others to consume and more closely aligns with the delivery model from the underlying Cloud vendor. In the authors' view, the role of IT needs to change in this new world. IT should not be building and operating this suite of services itself, as it may have done within a traditional tower model. IT should be presenting up these underlying capabilities as a set of easy-to-consume services. IT is now a shop, not a manufacturer.

It's important to match the portfolio of services closely that you want to provide to the services presented by the underlying platform. This is one of the (many) reasons why a multi-Cloud approach presents significant additional complexity. How do you map the items within your service portfolio to common services exposed by the underlying Clouds? Whilst VMs may be easy, as you get higher up the stack the differences become greater. SQL Azure and Amazon RDS provide the same kind of service, but the implementation (including performance tiers and pricing models) vary greatly.

You will also need to consider the process you go through to "approve" underlying Cloud services at the time you onboard them into your portfolio of services. You will need to build governance and compliance shims around them. You may support SQL Azure, but only if Transparent Data Encryption is turned on. Your SQL Azure Offer will therefore be a standard SQL Azure service, with that setting enabled and enforced.

Provisioning

Giving users access to your Cloud(s) is central to the effective operation of your Digital Operating Model. It comes with a fine and delicate balance, however.

How your users get access to a Cloud environment is one of the most contentious and hotly debated issues with Digital Operating Models. Cloud is automated and self-service. That is one of its defining characteristics. Nevertheless, uncontrolled access directly to the underlying Cloud environment presents serious difficulties for others. How are we going to control this? How are we going to secure this? How are we going to financially account for this? In the everlasting contention between agility and control, provisioning is the tip of the arrow. We want users to have quick and simple access. At the same time, we must enforce policy and governance.

Creating a Landing Zone

The first step to provision, is to build the underlying environment you're going to provision in to. In the past we have called these Azure Foundations, Virtual Datacenters or Azure Scaffold. Today, we refer to them as Landing Zones.

For details of building your Landing Zone, visit:
https://aka.ms/adopt/landingzone

Within a Landing Zone will be a core set of capabilities, networking access control, and templates. For the purposes of this we need only assume that we now have a core set of services available to us. We'll talk more about the services that would be deployed into a Landing Zone in the next two chapters on security and tooling.

Once we have this Landing Zone, we can create environments to sit alongside it which we can make available to product teams. We can then authorize that team to perform a set of actions, subject to the governance controls baked into the Landing Zone.

This is a useful place to interact with your service catalogue. Instead of individual configuration items in the catalogue, you can allow users to provision an entire "Cloud Environment" connected to a Landing Zone. During the provisioning process you collect information from the user, such as:

- Details of the owner
- The project code
- The cost code
- Information security classification of the data
- The service wrap / operational requirements for the environment
- Other pertinent information

This information can then be used to deploy the Cloud environment automatically. At the same time, it can set up the access control to the environment. Specific policies can be deployed on to the environment, such as tagging and cost allocation.

There are several ways to deploy these environments automatically. Some organizations choose to treat an environment as a resource group. They set up policy and access control accordingly. Others choose to deploy a complete Azure subscription. There are several factors to consider in making the choice.

Once a user has access to one of these Cloud environments, you need to build a set of mechanisms for things to make use of them. Different actors who will require access to these services in different ways.

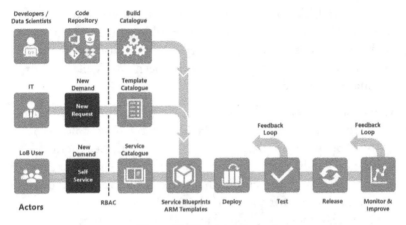

Figure 13 - Provisioning paths

Developers will want to consume these services from automated pipelines. They will therefore want to be presented with a set of curated "building blocks" which can be composed into templates within their deployment pipelines. These pipelines will execute many times over. You might present these to your users as NuGet packages which they can download and embed into their applications. You might house the templates in the same repositories that the developers are using.

IT administrators will likely want to go to a curated set of templates. They can use these to create artefacts or resources as a one-off operation as and when they are required. These would typically be made available within the Azure Portal or from PowerShell.

End users will want access to a simple to use, intuitive web interface to request new services, such as a Power BI license.

Whichever route "customers" of the service line take, the same automation, the same release process and the same monitoring and improvement should take place.

Service Catalogue

In an ITIL-based view of the world, there is only one entry point to services. That is the service catalogue. ITIL defines each of the services which users can consume. It gives them a shop from where they can obtain them. Do you want a VM? Sure, select one of the options below. Do you want a database? No problem, we have some available for you. The service catalogue can define workflows, scripts, approval steps – everything a user could possibly want. These will all have varying degrees of automation behind the scenes. It all sounds perfect, doesn't it? Well unfortunately, not quite!

Service catalogues can still play an interesting and important part of your Cloud provisioning process. However, the huge volume of items available within a platform such as Azure makes them incredibly unwieldy. Consider for a start that there are over 200 Azure services. Then remember that there could be several dozen variants and options for each one. For VMs alone (one of the Azure services), there are more than 150 different ranges and sizes to choose from. Over 150! Every week a new VM size is launched. Every few months a new range comes online as hardware is deployed in the datacenters. Each type of VM has specific rules as to what disks, networks or other services it can attach or connect to. Trying to maintain a mapping between your own service catalogue and the underlying platform is like bailing out an ocean with a bucket. It is theoretically possible, given enough time and enough resource. But it is as close to impossible as you can get. It is also a never-ending job. Suppose you managed to map the range of services available and create deployment scripts for each one; by the time you had finished, half of them would be out of date.

There is another disadvantage to basing your provisioning on a service catalogue. It flies in the face of the automation that the Cloud delivers. A service catalogue is usually on the web. A user searches for an item and deploys it. Suppose your application has many different items – VMs, databases, and so on. It is boring and laborious to deploy them one by one to each environment. Some organizations do, however, choose to make a small selection of configuration items available via a service catalogue. That might include a dozen VMs and a couple of database SKUs. That offers a few easy-to-consume items so that less technically-savvy users can get up and running. Later on, these users can be introduced to the wonders of templates and automation.

A world built on code

Instead of providing users access to provision individual services, a better approach is to construct a library of templates and scripts.

These can then serve as a useful abstraction between your users and the underlying Cloud platform to enforce your own security standards and policies.

Using Azure DevOps, you can create a repository of all these assets. You can combine a set of Azure Resource Manager (ARM) templates, Azure Policies and Azure Desired State Configurations (DSCs).

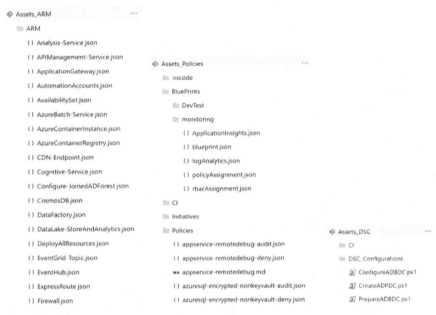

Figure 14 - Code libraries

As an added benefit of using Azure DevOps, you can run a set of automated tests, including the Secure DevOps Toolkit to proactively make a set of recommendations to keep your scripts and templates secure and in line with Microsoft's best practice. Users can then execute these templates directly, or they can compose them into a pipeline of automated actions.

Incident

Incident management is as important within your Digital Operating Model as it was on premises. Things will still go wrong. You need a process to govern this. A move to the Cloud, however, affords far more opportunities to automate this incident management approach.

Your incident management process will typically have a couple of different variants. This depends on whether it is a response to an incident on an infrastructure-based (Mode 1) environment or a code-based (Mode 2) environment.

In a Mode 1 world, incident management will still take a feed from an alerting platform. This will either invoke a run book or pass this alert on to a technician for resolution These human resolver groups will undertake work broadly analogous to the work that they performed on premises. They will make use of problem management tools to identify, triage and ultimately resolve these incidents. Your problem management tooling will necessarily evolve to offer more automated resolutions. Rather than describing a set of steps which can be performed to resolve the incident, they may reference a script or a runbook which can be executed instead.

Within your application incident model, you will be able to make use of extensive automation. The idea is that is it easier, quicker and less risky to re-run a deployment pipeline to build a known-working environment of something rather than attempt to fix a broken one. If this doesn't work, you can roll-back to the last release. It's possible that there might be a bug lurking within the newest release.

Whether it's an incident on your infrastructure or an incident on your applications, the amount of data and telemetry that you're able to pull from the underlying platform should make it much easier to spot trends and reduce resolution time. Many organizations are now starting to build sophisticated machine learning models. These can predict incidents in advance. They make far more detailed recommendations to resolver groups about suggested steps to take.

As you design your incident management approach and SLAs it's vital you consider compound SLAs. Your team may have an SLA of 15 minutes to respond to and triage an incident. If the issue turns out to be with your Cloud provider, the clock on their SLA only starts ticking when the incident is escalated to them. They may take another 15 minutes to respond and triage. Ensure you don't over-commit in terms of SLAs given the dependencies you will have on others in this new world.

Change and risk

As with incident management, change and risk management need to be re-imagined in our new operating model. Change management is probably the most affected of the service management processes. You must come to terms with the fact you no longer have operational responsibility for the whole environment. The move from build-and-run to consuming services is transformational for change management.

The underlying service fabric for many of your services is constantly changing. You will be able to manage some of them. Others you will be told about in time to prepare. But some changes just happen. Microsoft is very good at warning about upcoming changes that they expect to affect customers. Examples are a service reaching end of life or being deprecated. They will give you several months' notice and suggest an upgrade or migration path. They will often circulate a change such as an uplift to mailbox size in Office 365. Likewise, with a change of a licensing plan. It is the responsibility of the in-house IT team or the service provider to keep up to date with these changes. Changes to the underlying platform are not exposed. They are run internally by the Cloud-hosting provider.

You will need to look at your environment in groups of services. There are the services you control such as your VM guest operating systems and SQL servers. They can be managed in a traditional way. But services you consume such as Office 365 and PaaS services in Azure will need to be treated as third party. You will have little or no say over when changes take place. You will, however, be notified of these changes so you can warn staff.

Everything we have covered so far is challenging. But it is achievable for your change process. What does this look like in a Mode 2 world? In Mode 2 change is the whole point. You can make thousands of micro changes a week. This is the source of business benefit that Mode 2 workloads deliver. In such a model you can't possibly hope to govern these workloads through a formal change process. Therefore, these workloads need to have strong testing and rollback baked into the deployment process. We cover this in more detail in the DevOps chapter. For now, we will only say that you should educate the service organization about their future. They need to get a feel for how things will look as you progress on your journey to Cloud adoption.

Capacity Management

Capacity management has a lesser, yet still important role within your Digital Operating Model. Capacity management no longer needs to have regard to physical equipment. We no longer need to concern ourselves with the procurement and deployment of physical servers and storage arrays. For all intents and purposes, we can treat the Cloud as delivering infinite capacity. There are, however, a couple of caveats to this approach.

This first caveat is if you are delivering a hyper-scale service within the Cloud. If you typically need to spin up thousands of cores on a variable basis you may hit constraint limits. Even hyperscale Clouds only have a certain amount of excess capacity within the platform. If you think you might fall into this category, engage with your Cloud provider to understand how you can pay for the ability to deliver these kinds of peak expansion.

The other interesting dimension is reserved instances. We covered these within the financial governance chapter. Reserved instances allow organizations to pre-commit to certain levels of usage. Instead of purchasing a server by the minute, if you know the workload will stay static for a year or three years, consider committing to this. The savings will be substantial. In order to assess these forward-looking capacity demands you need – you guessed it – capacity management. Don't get too hung up on reserved instances at the beginning and certainly don't commit to them until your given workload has been running a month or two. Until you can see how your application performs in the Cloud you don't know what size of servers you need. You don't know whether or not you might in fact be better off with a variable compute model.

The new "run" business

Major changes are required to your service management organization to support this new world of change and automation. Barriers must be broken down. Teams need to come together and collaborate more. New service façades on top of SaaS services must be introduced. Platform services teams need to be born.

For an introduction to how to reorganize your teams, visit:
https://aka.ms/adopt/organize

Consider a traditional service such as e-mail. A simplified view of your service management organization may look like this:

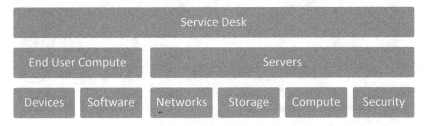

Figure 15 - Traditional support model

After moving to a service such as Office 365, your service management organization should turn into something like this:

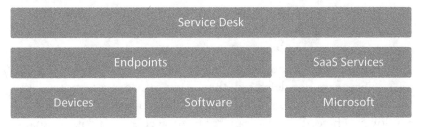

Figure 16 - SaaS support model

A simple change, but one a having profound impact. There is now a symbiotic link between your service organization and that of your new Cloud provider. We discussed this in chapter 8. You no longer have access to server teams to diagnose and fix issues with the underlying infrastructure supporting your business. Your Cloud provider now employs these people. What's important is the interface between you and them.

You may choose to interface directly with these providers. Or you may choose to work via a Cloud solutions provider. Whichever way you chose to solve this challenge, it will be regularly tested within your new run organization. You must ensure that you have access to the right people, as quickly as possible. Tight SLAs are required to deliver these new services to the users.

Support for internal line of business applications becomes even further removed from what it is today. At present, there is a clear separation between the development and onboarding teams on the one hand, and the operations team on the other. There are defined hand-over mechanisms.

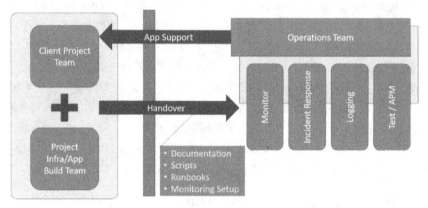

Figure 17 - Traditional application support model © Servian

But this disjointed approach to application delivery is slow. There can be a delay of four to six weeks in getting an application from the project team to the operations team. When issues do arise, there can be a them and us conflict between the two teams. Once the project team has delivered, they often refuse any responsibility for issues in production. This increases the complexity of the handover. The operations team try to foresee every problem that might arise later. They want to satisfy themselves that the application is completely ready. In our new run world these teams come together. They become two sides of the same coin, working collaboratively together:

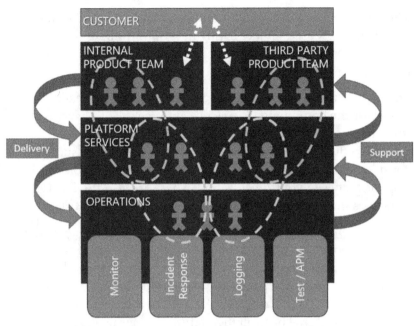

Figure 18 - Next generation applications support © Servian

Key to this new support model is the platform services team. This team is the special sauce. They are the ninjas, the automation specialists. This team mediates the work of the applications team and the work of the operations team. They support both internal applications teams and third-party ones. They work between the two worlds.

Structuring your new teams

There are several approaches to structuring your new teams. Within the Cloud Adoption Framework, Microsoft suggests at least two teams. A Cloud Adoption team and a Cloud Governance team.

Figure 19 - Cloud adoption and governance teams

For more information, visit:

https://aka.ms/adopt/organize/establishteams

These two teams will naturally compete. That is OK. The Adoption team will be focused on identifying new opportunities to leverage Cloud technologies. The Governance team will be focused on keeping them safe and secure.

For each of these teams, you can choose the center of excellence model, or the community of practice approach. Both have had some measure of success in organizations today. There are many aspects to the choice of model for your organization. Issues to consider include your funding models and the overall roles and responsibilities in your organization. There are also the DevOps principles that will mandate the reduction or removal of silos.

The community of practice approach is suitable for organizations that are product and green fields based. The development teams will complete the building of the new capability. They will ensure that it's made ready for production. They will also ensure that it is clear what the developers will look after and what operations will be responsible for. They will then return to their product teams.

A center of excellence style platform services team is suitable in other situations. For example, in a large enterprise, development or product teams could appoint members on a more permanent basis. That would allow them to lay out their requirements and support the ongoing provision of services.

For an example RACI matrix for these teams, visit:
https://aka.ms/adopt/organize/raci

Over time, there will be a requirement to align these teams to your existing central IT teams. This is not without risk. The central IT team must come to the party with a growth mindset. The worst situation is where these teams gravitate back to traditional approaches. They might fall back on traditional ways of doing things to "align" with the greater IT service management universe. You must not let them. Central IT needs to mimic the new model, not vice versa.

Starting from the top

All these fundamental changes to your service management organization must start from the top. They must start from the beginning too. As project/innovation and operations teams come closer together, so do their reporting lines. Digital initiatives within organizations often drive a lot of this change. But they must operate closely with operations. Have you ever heard about a digital team who decreed PaaS-first, while the operations team didn't officially support PaaS in production? You come across it time and again. There are two poles pulling in opposite directions – two organizations without a common strategy or goal.

You want to get your service management organization firing on all cylinders and adequately supporting the business. To do so you must dissolve the fiefdoms. Everyone needs to be on the same page within the one organization.

For more information on dissolving the fiefdoms, visit:
https://aka.ms/adopt/organize/antipatterns

There are different approaches to achieve this. The simplest is to make sure everyone has the same reporting lines. Several roles can perform this function. It might be a Chief Information Officer (CIO), a Chief Technology Officer (CTO), or a Head of Digital (HOD). It doesn't so much matter the title given to this person. What matters is that this person heads a joint organization. They must ensure that the different parts of the business play nicely together. This is essential if you want to become truly digital.

Chapter

Access Control, Security and Policy

The need for security often kills the quest for innovation

Haresh Sippy (1946 -), Industrialist

Rethinking your attitude to risk

S ECURITY, security, security! Never has one word struck so much fear in the minds of CIOs, CEOs and boards of directors. It's a trump card that can be played in an almost arbitrary way in any situation, but it is often played to achieve the wrong result.

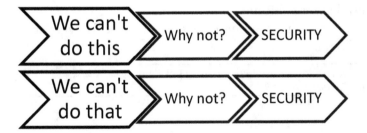

In any conflict between security and innovation, security wins.

Security is, of course, incredibly important. You only need to watch the news to hear about the latest data breach, the latest ransomware, the latest exploit discovered in something you use every day. In the words of James Rozoff: *"[Although] security is an illusion ... it is a pleasant one."* Security is ultimately about risk management. What level of risk are you prepared to accept as an organization? What odds are you prepared to place a bet on? A one in a million chance of something happening, or a one in several billion? What damage might arise from the theoretical threat we are protecting against?

For many years, security was the main reason organizations gave for their failure to adopt public Cloud services. We can't use service xyz because [insert some reason related to security]. Over recent years, most of this fear, uncertainty and doubt (FUD) has melted away. People now admit that the security delivered by most public Cloud providers is actually superior to the security that can be delivered on-premises. But many still don't admit it, and still believe the Cloud-is-not-Secure mantra. To those readers, you may as well stop reading here. We wish you good luck. The rest of this chapter is addressed to those who are willing to trust that the public Cloud can be configured to deliver security – security that is at least as good, if not better than what is available on premises. You will now want to learn how to take advantage of the security that is on offer from the public Cloud. In this chapter we will explore the things you need to take into consideration and the questions you should ask. In that way you should be able to deliver something at least as secure as you can deliver today, and more likely, more secure.

Access Control

Access control is authentication plus authorization. That is to say, identity is the most important ingredient in the recipe for what are you allowed to do.

For a guide on where to start with your identity baseline, visit:
https://aka.ms/adopt/gov/identity

Identity as your chain of command

A central part of any Digital Operating Model is the definition and implementation of a Cloud identity provider (IdP). Your operating model depends everywhere and in every scenario on the system that identifies who you are and/or what group of users you belong to.

In the on-premises world, Active Directory is the source of this identity almost exclusively. Every user and every service have an Active Directory credential. In the Cloud an equivalent of Active Directory is needed. But instead of authenticating and authorizing access to devices and legacy applications, a Cloud identity controls access to Cloud platforms and services. A Cloud IdP is a single sign-on (SSO) platform on steroids.

There are several Cloud IdPs on the market today. They include Okta, Auth0, Centrify, and Azure Active Directory. Each has its pros and cons and an associated commercial model. Most deliver some form of Active Directory federation. The first thing to do is undertake an evaluation of these IdP platforms. Look at what they support and ask the smart questions. Choose the one that will work for you. Then go ahead and deploy it as quickly as you can.

Deploying a Cloud IdP can be straightforward, or it can be complicated. If you're linking it to your existing on-premises Active Directory, additional work may be required. You may need to tidy up your current environment since you might not have followed best practice. Your environment might have evolved over time. You might have acquired or divested organizations which form part of your Active Directory forest but are not good neighbors.

Although sometimes daunting, this work must be done. Your identity model forms the core of your Digital Operating Model. Take the time to do it right. The good news for Office 365 users is that you already have a Cloud IdP. You may not realize it, but the page where you log on to Office 365 is in fact Azure Active Directory.

Multi-factor authentication

Once you have established your IdP, you need to build the controls which surround it. Multi-factor authentication (MFA) used to be the preserve of the biggest organizations and those most paranoid about security. With the Cloud, this capability has been opened to everyone. The need for expensive hardware access tokens or proprietary solutions has gone. It's typically built in, out of the box. You now have the choice of rolling it out to all users or to a subset. Another option is to base it on a set of criteria. Such criteria might include whether the user is at home or at work, or whether suspicious activity has been detected. Agree your rules and incorporate these into your Digital Operating Model.

Single sign-on

MFA was the exception rather than the rule. The same is true of single sign-on. It used to be a nice-to-have option. It was something you did if it wasn't excruciatingly difficult or expensive. Within a Digital Operating Model, it's a virtual necessity.

We discussed earlier the requirements you place on service providers as part of a procurement exercise. SSO support must be a major factor in your decision. SSO standards such as OAuth have proliferated. And so, finding a service provider who can participate within your identity realm is relatively straightforward.

Many Cloud IdPs have support for hundreds if not thousands of pre-built integrations. At the time of writing, Azure Active Directory supports more than 2,500 SaaS-based applications.

Joiners, movers and leavers

JML is an important process to introduce into your Digital Operating Model. A JML process describes the steps to be taken when an employee starts at your organization, changes role or departs. Giving people access to systems, changing their access, or withdrawing access all have serious security implications.

The work to be done depends on the kinds of Cloud services and Cloud IdP you are using. It also depends on the setup of your single sign-on access to each system. Typically, single sign-on is based on identity federation and a token-based chain of control. A target system uses your main credentials to provide access. For these services, your JML process will be fairly streamlined. You will create or disable a user account. This will be done either within your on-premises Active Directory, or directly within your Cloud IdP. Users can be moved into, out of, or between security groups. This is not very different from the way you do it on premises today.

In some scenarios, relying services have their own instance of a user's identity. This will be piggybacked onto the main credential. Enabling or disabling a user's primary credential doesn't necessarily enable or disable the secondary account. Moving a user between security groups might not modify their access within these systems. For such scenarios, you will probably need to increase the complexity and tooling that your JML process leverages. Suitable technologies include Microsoft Identity Manager (MIM). There are others. Azure Active Directory Premium (AADP) also has prebuilt functionality to achieve this for Cloud services such as Workday.

Best practice for your cloud IdP

At this point you have your Cloud IdP enabled and deployed and your users synced with it. Now you can enable federated access to your Cloud services, such as Office 365 and Azure. The best practices you have employed on-premises for years apply just as well in the Cloud. One such practice is to always use security groups rather than individual users when giving access to operations within Cloud environments. Leveraging inheritance and hierarchies is an example. Start with a broader definition of users, then narrow it down. Definitions of users and the kinds of operations you want to allow them to undertake become more and more specific. These concepts are no different in the Cloud and should be the same in your Digital Operating Model.

For more detailed guidance on the set of Azure tools available for Identity, visit: *https://aka.ms/adopt/gov/identity/toolchain*

IdP and your Cloud platform

For SaaS applications, your identity model will be relatively straightforward. It will broadly mirror the way users are provided with access to on-premises applications today. For your Cloud platform (IaaS/PaaS) the complexity increases somewhat. Your IaaS and PaaS layers will contain the actual nuts and bolts of your underlying applications. This includes the servers and services which compose them. You will typically have multiple environments for each of your applications, including test/dev, UAT and production. Differing user access rights will apply to each environment and to sets of services.

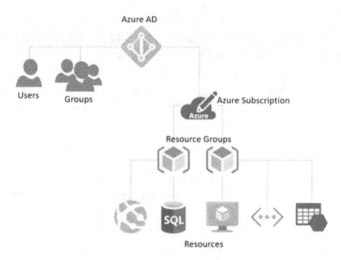

Figure 20 - Azure security model

The concept of an environment may also change. With traditional infrastructure, you have pre-provisioned environments. They are set up in advance and into them servers and security groups are deployed. You will still have these kinds of environments in the Cloud. But you may also introduce ephemeral environments. An ephemeral environment is one which is created and destroyed on the fly, often at a high rate. The environment will be declarative. That is, it is self-describing and encapsulated. It will be based on a set of templates and scripts which can be automatically deployed. An application won't be deployed into the given environment. Instead a new test and dev, UAT, or production environment will be created. This will be done on the fly, specifically for this application. It's a very different concept from what you have been used to.

What makes up an environment may also be different in this new Cloud world. Traditionally, an environment might include a large set of assets, including servers, networks, VLANs, switches, and so on. In the new Cloud world, an environment might just be a defined group of services, such as a resource group.

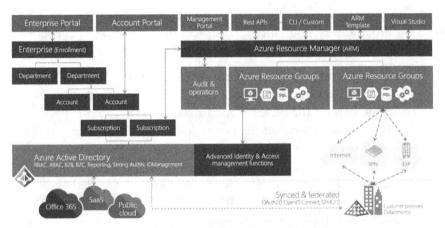

Figure 21 - Azure role-based access hierarchy

However your environments are being deployed, you need to make sure you have sufficient identity controls to secure and manage them. Typically, this will comprise owners and a set of differing roles beneath them.

For more detailed guidance on RBAC controls, visit:
https://aka.ms/adopt/ready/manageaccess

Security

The security of your Cloud environment is all-encompassing. This is a broad topic. Your approach to security will involve several individuals and teams from across your organization.

Normally security covers physical, infrastructure, networks and VM/apps. After moving to the Cloud, you no longer need to be concerned about the physical and infrastructure layers. Instead you can focus your efforts on the network and VM/app layer. Your security design will not necessarily form part of your Digital Operating Model. But the principles and vendor solutions (native vs third-party) that you will enforce do need to be agreed and planned. They will have far-reaching implications for things such as support, performance and availability.

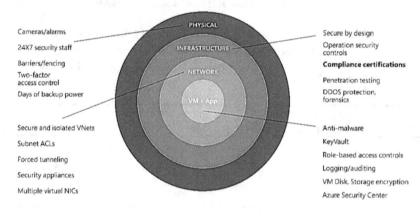

Figure 22 - Trust and control model

Perimeter security

You need to protect your perimeter first. That is no different from a traditional on-premises environment. Azure contains several capabilities built natively into the platform to help supply perimeter security. Among these are Azure's DDoS Protection and Mitigation service and its Firewall service.

There are also third-party security products on the Azure marketplace. Among these are Palo Alto, Barracuda, and Checkpoint. There are others. These third-party appliances are useful when designing a hybrid perimeter security model. Especially so if you have physical or virtual appliances from these vendors deployed on-premises today. In this model, Azure becomes just another datacenter with ingress and egress points needing to be protected.

Customers who have deployed ExpressRoute have additional options and requirements for their Azure environments. An ExpressRoute circuit is a private link between the Microsoft datacenter(s) and your existing offices and datacenters. Some customers chose to route all their traffic into or out of Azure and Office 365 via this connection. In this way, all traffic can be inspected on-premises via an appliance. The exceptions are certain whitelisted internet services such as Windows Update.

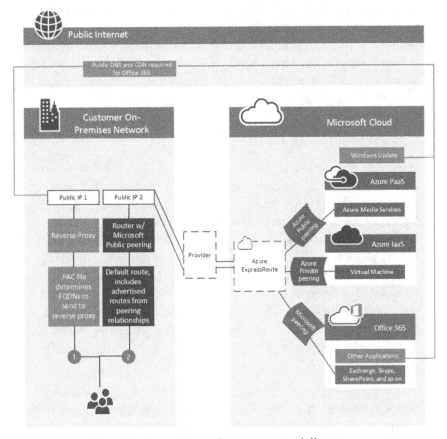

Figure 23 - Azure ExpressRoute conceptual diagram

Leveraging ExpressRoute and forced tunneling can have significant impact, reducing your bandwidth and network capacity. It is something that should be carefully considered.

You will also need a web application firewall (WAF) if you are exposing web applications to the internet directly from inside Azure. A WAF delivers more than a standard firewall. It does more than answer the question: Can I connect on this port? A WAF understands the detail of web traffic. It inspects traffic for inappropriate behaviors and attacks by malicious third parties. WAFs protect against common attack vectors such as SQL injection attacks.

Dedicated web application firewalls used to be expensive to procure and to configure. In Azure, they are even simpler than deploying a VM. Azure has its own WAF capability built in called Azure Front Door. Alternatively, there are third parties offering solutions out of the box. Both allow extensive configuration and control of web traffic entering your environment.

Internal security

Now that your perimeter security is in place, you need to ensure that you enforce appropriate separation of network segments internally. This is something you may have done using VLANs or by enforcing security between different subnets. In the Cloud, this is still what you do. Only now you have a different set of tools and services. Instead of VLANs, we have virtual networks in Azure. Each virtual network is assigned a pool of IP addresses and a set of routes and connections through to other virtual networks. In Azure you set network security groups. This is like setting ACLs on a firewall to control traffic between network segments, These NSGs can either be applied to VNETs or to resources which attach to a virtual network.

Some organizations choose to deploy third-party appliances to control the flow of traffic between virtual networks. That is in the same way as they control ingress and egress from a Cloud environment. Others choose to use native capabilities.

VMs and apps

Security at the VM and application layer is complex. It is a separate topic that requires to be considered in depth. Each application will present a bespoke requirement for connectivity. The approach you take to secure each one will be different.

The main issue for your Digital Operating Model is not the specifics. It is to define your overall approach to securing your VMs and applications. Many organizations moving to the Cloud take the opportunity to apply additional controls. They might not have been able or willing to apply such controls before. These might include:

- Host-based security / firewalls
- Enforcing IPSEC-based connections to VMs
- Deploying advanced antivirus and host-based intrusion detection

It is unnecessary for your Digital Operating Model to get into details at a VM by VM or app by app level. But it does need to include some high-level objectives and controls. These are the controls you would like to be introduced. This leads neatly on to the next chapter about monitoring, management and automation.

Azure Security Center

Now you've followed best practice and baked security into every part of your Azure environment. How do you police this and check that your environment is configured correctly? The answer is the Azure Security Center (ASC). Despite being a Cloud service, ASC can provide visibility across your entire hybrid estate. It can help manage policy compliance. It can also perform security assessments and make proactive recommendations on issues to be addressed and resolved. Find out how you can leverage these capabilities as part of your Digital Operating Model.

Microsoft Threat Protection

We have been looking at the work to secure your new Azure datacenter. There are other tools and capabilities to help secure your end-to-end Microsoft Cloud environment. Microsoft Threat Protection (MTP) is one of the newer ones. MTP provides a view of an organization's overall threat landscape. Administrators can easily spot new threats and attacks. MTP pulls data from numerous services and combines them for viewing on a centralized dashboard – such services as Office 365 Threat Intelligence, Azure Active Directory Identity Protection, and Windows Advanced Threat Protection.

The most interesting aspect of Microsoft Threat Protection is the sophisticated artificial intelligence baked into it. New and unseen threats can be spotted and stopped in real time. Embedding MTP in your Digital Operating Model will provide additional security and assurance for your Microsoft Cloud environment.

Microsoft Threat Protection also hooks into Microsoft's brand new Security Incident and Event Management (SIEM) product, Sentinel. Sentinel is a class-leading Cloud-native SIEM which provides limitless storage and analytics for security signals from across your organization.

Policy

One of the most fundamental shifts within an effective Digital Operating Model is to move from a process-based model of security and compliance to a policy-based one. What do we mean by this?

Policy and compliance are one of the three bedrocks behind Govern within the Cloud Adoption Framework for Azure. For more information, visit: *https://aka.ms/adopt/gov/corporatepolicy*

Today, most organizations' approach to security and compliance is to leverage processes. Detailed processes will be drawn up for every aspect of IT security and compliance. These processes will describe everything that has to happen, step by step for an application or service to be approved and deployed into production. This process will typically involve dozens of signoffs, design committees, accreditations and more. This process-based approach is largely successful and ensures that there are many eyes on things as they go through the process. Multiple points to catch bad designs or people trying to do things which would impact on security or compliance. There are, unfortunately, three major challenges with this approach:

Firstly, it is highly reliant on people. As we all know, people make mistakes.

Secondly, especially in terms of the successful adoption of a Digital Operating Model, it is slow, laborious and complex. Trying to build a process to govern the use and deployment of any of the hundreds of services available within Azure verges on the impossible.

Thirdly, and most critically, it's very difficult to demonstrate compliance with a process-based approach to security and compliance. Sure, we can say we have a process. We can say that of course everyone follows the said process. But, as we know, those two statements alone are not always enough to placate accreditors. What we need is a deterministic methodology to demonstrate compliance. Consequently, we suggest a different route. Enter policy.

With a policy-based approach to security and compliance we switch the model on its head. What if, instead of describing a process which enforces checks against controls, we could describe the controls themselves. Rather than having a technical design review to check that there were sufficient separation of controls, we had a policy which could describe it. Rather than have a committee check that all aspects of the application are deployed into a certain sovereign geography, let us have a policy that enforced it. That is the core of a policy-based approach.

With this policy-based approach we have several significant advantages:

Firstly, we can start to achieve the balance between agility and control which is the centerpiece of our Digital Operating Model. With a policy-based approach the control can be expressed as policy, not a series of steps in a process. An environment can be evaluated against a declarative policy in seconds. A process could take days or weeks. Once we are comfortable that the policy is enforcing the control, we can start to scale back the process. We can even, once we're really comfortable, do away with much or all of the process. The policy serves as a set of guardrails to keep everyone safe. We no longer need to keep people safe with process.

The second and even more powerful aspect of this policy-based approach is its ability to demonstrate, deterministically, whether your environment is compliant or not. If our control is expressed as a series of policies, we can say definitively that we are either in, or out, of compliance. We don't need to even describe a process anymore. The fact that the policy is there and that everything is compliant demonstrates that we can rest safe in the knowledge that all is in order.

Creating your policies

The native tool to achieve this is Azure Policy. Policy is the mechanism you use to control and enforce the provisioning and ongoing security and management of resources within your environment. Policies allow you to define what good looks like. They define the settings, configuration, placement and many other rules that apply to your Cloud(s). Some of these policies will be simple to conceive.

- I want all my data stored within the European Union – or maybe specifically in England.
- I want all data to be encrypted at rest.
- I must be able to allocate usage charges to departments/cost codes.

Some policies will be more complex. If this and this and this are true, I want you to do this, so long as something else is not true, in which case I want you to do that.

Policies should, wherever possible, align with security requirements. They should also, wherever possible, match external security standards, such as PCI DSS. In this way, you can demonstrate security compliance through policy compliance.

Azure has wide support for policies through Azure Policy. Azure Policy allows you to define complex sets of rules which can be enforced at both provisioning time and ongoing. They can require that, for instance, any VM being placed into any given environment should have certain agents deployed and configured. They can require that transparent data encryption is enabled for any SQL Azure instance.

Azure also has capabilities provided by Desired State Config (DSC). This allows detailed configuration patterns to be attached to Azure services. The patterns apply on deployment. They also maintain compliance with the configuration over time. There are also popular open source solutions such as Chef, Puppet and

Ansible. They can be made available within your Azure environment. They are useful for organizations that use a lot of open source platforms. Also check out the newly released Azure Deployment Manager.

For details of building policy into your Landing Zone, visit:
https://aka.ms/adopt/ready/gov

Third-party products also exist in this space such as Palo Alto Evident, NeuVector, DivvyCloud and Dome 9. These products can span multiple Clouds. These products allow you to set policies which can be applied to environments after the fact. They support several external standards. They are also not native, however.

You might already have an environment where you hadn't deployed Azure Policy or DSC. But you now want to bring it into compliance. You might not want rigid policies. You might want to allow developers greater freedom but have guardrails in place to keep them on the straight and narrow. You might run other products as well as inbuilt capabilities. This will allow you to enforce compliance and then independently demonstrate it.

Whatever approach you take to policy, make it your central platform. Make it the single point of authority. Keep it as fully managed source code within your software development platform. Protect it. Nurture it. Covet it. It's now the front line between you and the bad guys and girls. You need it, and you need it to work. It's quite a significant change in mindset, but this one simple paradigm shift has profound impact and is one of the central themes of your Digital Operating Model.

Chapter

Monitoring, Management and Automation

The first rule of any technology used in a business is that automation applied to an efficient operation will magnify the efficiency. The second is that automation applied to an inefficient operation will magnify the inefficiency

Bill Gates (1955 -), Founder Microsoft Corporation

F OR those that have skipped ahead, one of the most powerful messages we have attempted to relay in the book so far is the need for automation in the Public Cloud. The authors are often asked to define what Cloud really means. The answer is typically something along the lines of the application of automation and software to tasks which were traditionally manual. That and very big datacenters! Connecting two network segments together used to involve a physical piece of wire. It's now a software command.

A Public Cloud fabric allows you to instruct the fabric programmatically to perform a task via an API call. This can be done from anywhere at any time through the magic of a software defined environment. An organization with a Digital Operating Model becomes a software defined business.

It is this critical thing which brings about the efficiency of delivering services from the public Cloud. But it is typically the operations function that benefits the most from automation.

It should be the aim of all businesses to run as much of their IT operations as possible using tools rather than people. In so doing, staff members will be freed to add value higher up the business value chain.

We have referred several times to the Gartner concepts of Mode 1 and Mode 2. With Public Cloud there is the option to meet somewhere in the middle with what we might call Mode 1.5. In this mode you can automate the management of Mode 1 workloads in something approaching a pseudo-Mode 2 manner. To put it simply, you don't have to transform your workloads to transform your service management function.

Clearly, the more a workload is native to the Cloud, the easier it is to apply sophisticated automation. In the DevOps chapter we'll talk about how to achieve this for software development. For now, we will look at how this applies to Mode 1 workloads and how you can begin to move towards a Cloud-native Operating Model.

Take the more traditional workloads such as COTS applications installed and running on VMs in public Cloud. These can also benefit from the type of automated processes which Cloud can provide. To illustrate this, let's take as an example a simple three tier application. Our fictitious application has a presentation layer on a web service running on server A. It also has an application layer with some functional binaries that do "a thing" on server B. Finally, there is a database on server C.

Using Cloud-based tools you can monitor the health of the guest operating system. You can also monitor the primary workload running on each server's guest operating system. In addition to that you can get telemetry from the Azure fabric for the services you are consuming to run these VMs. This telemetry includes the compute object, the storage account, the end point, the network card and so on. This information from the Azure fabric can be blended with the log information coming from the guest operating system. You now have a good understanding of the state of the component parts. Microsoft provides tools such as Log Analytics and Service Map. These components can be stitched together, providing a single application level view of health.

Now, we can imagine a situation where a component is in trouble or the guest operating system is throwing warnings out. Using Log Analytics you can create alerts that query the log data. In turn the alerts trigger automated run books in Azure. These can execute commands on the fabric and the guest operating system as required.

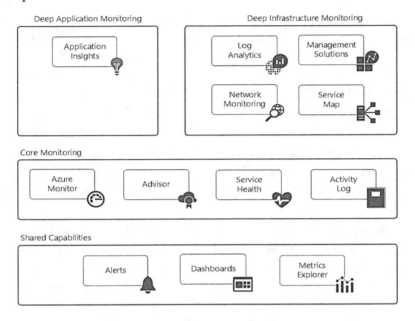

Figure 24 - Monitoring map

With these simple tools, we can now script almost any configuration change on both the Public Cloud fabric and the guest operating systems. This opens the doors to a whole new world of support options.

Monitor / Signal / Telemetry

Key to all this happening is a common and consistent toolchain. Organizations have over the years accumulated a vast array of tools from different providers. Each delivers a set of capabilities to monitor, collect telemetry from and manage an overall environment. These include storage arrays, network performance, and a dozen others – disparate and disconnected.

Often these tools were considered best of breed by various analysts. Quadrants, waves – each operated very effectively with the set of tasks it was asked to perform. Time goes by though, and the tide is shifting.

Now a new set of tools and services present themselves. Tools and services which you might describe as Cloud-native or alternatively platform-native. They are tools and services which are part of the underlying Cloud itself.

Microsoft has given particular focus to this area and has worked hard to build a set of services to replicate its traditional on-premises software. Many organizations today leverage the Microsoft management suite, System Center. The new set of capabilities which are built into the Microsoft Cloud build upon these foundations. Yet they have been completely rewritten for the Cloud.

What we need within our new Digital Operating Model is a holistic approach to monitoring and alerting. A centralized approach. One that leverages that common and consistent, but now platform-native set of tools.

In the immediate term our focus will stay on VMs, as these are likely to be the first workloads which you onboard into the Cloud. Azure Desired State Configuration allows you to define a set of configurations and tools to deploy onto machines as they are migrated. Deploying Azure Monitor and its underlying Log Analytics provides an extensive set of capabilities which you can leverage out of the box. There is full, native integration into Azure Security Center and Azure Sentinel.

This simple set of tools provides an end-to-end, enterprise grade setup, for a fraction of what your equivalent on premises toolchain costs today. Whilst there will invariably not be 100 percent feature parity to what you might have today, the gap is closing rapidly. If you haven't got something approaching this today, you now do. For very little extra investment.

For further reading on monitoring, visit:

https://aka.ms/adopt/ready/monitor

Alerting and triggers

Once you've agreed on what your toolchain will be, you need to build an alert management workflow. An alert is raised when a service breaches a defined threshold. The monitoring tool is then told to act in some way. These alerts can be simple metric-based counters, like those for CPU, Memory and Disk usage. Or they may be more complex such as a service fault.

It is even possible to get very sophisticated and map a higher-level service like an application to its component parts. This will reveal the impact of a given component on the overall health of the system.

These alerts then need wiring into your service management tool. You'll need to understand what these alerts mean and write logic to handle them. Some may be background noise, some indicative of an actual issue where intervention is called for. In the same ways that we do on premises today, we need to correlate and understand the pattern of these alerts.

Initially, you will almost certainly undertake much of this work manually. Alerts will be routed to human resolver groups for investigation. As you and your tooling get more sophisticated you can begin to apply additional levels of intelligence and start to introduce automated remediation.

One of the significant advantages of leveraging Cloud-based tooling lies in the addition of services such as best practice analyzers. They can make proactive recommendations using the event information and alerts. Many can be automatically remediated, straight from the console.

Modern Management and Compliance

Monitoring and management need to extend from the Cloud to the edge. Devices accessing your central Cloud environment need to be governed, monitored and controlled to maintain your overall compliance position. With Windows 10, Microsoft can now apply the same native management experience to the edge.

This means an end of gold images. An end of "corporate approved devices". Now anyone can buy any Windows 10 machine that meets a certain specification and enroll it as part of the out of the box (OOB) experience. Users can simply sign in with a set of corporate Cloud credentials and the device builds itself to the corporate standard. With Windows Autopilot companies can also pre-enroll devices to force them to join Azure AD and Intune automatically.

With Cloud-enrolled devices, Windows now becomes "Windows as a Service". With this upgrade motion, Microsoft now assumes some of the responsibility for the build, deployment and service motion of endpoints. Rather than traditional three-year upgrade cycles, devices now stay up-to-date with the latest version of Windows.

Once in Intune, other policies and applications can be deployed and the Servicing Channel chosen. Intune is an always-on, internet-facing service. And so, every time a device connects to the internet it will check in with Intune and policy or updates will be deployed.

Scripting

Some of us have been in IT for a couple of decades. For us in the Unix/Linux team, scripting was a way of life. We lived in our BASH shell and crafted scripts. We used arcane commands like awk, grep, and sed to do all manner of things.

Microsoft brought in a Windows-based scripting language with the introduction of PowerShell v1.0 in 2006. This replicated abilities previously only enjoyed by Unix sysadmins. Now Windows-based sysadmins could automate repetitive tasks. They could assess or alter the configuration of servers and workstations which reduced the need for tools or compiled code. This move to scripting therefore started long before the Cloud became mainstream. Microsoft introduced the concept of a "core" server back in Windows Server 2008. No Windows Explorer shell was installed. All tasks were carried out using the Command Line Interface (CLI). Since then, all server operating systems have had this option. PowerShell went through several iterations before the decision was made in 2016 to take it multi-platform and open source. The Nano server option with 2016 and 2019, for example, can only be administered locally though PowerShell

When Microsoft developed the interfaces for both Azure and Office 365, it was no surprise therefore that they built them on PowerShell. The IT community now had a common language to administer everything. That includes a Windows desktop client, a server guest operating system, back office services like SQL server and Exchange. They could also administer the Cloud fabric these services run on, if they are being consumed from Azure and Office 365.

Microsoft also adopted JSON to transmit data describing types and attributes of services in Azure. PowerShell enables you to assess and change the configuration of items across the whole Cloud service stack. Add to that a descriptor file using the JSON standard and you can pretty much do anything you like. You no longer need to sit at a graphical interface. This approach is becoming the new normal.

The more you advance in the Cloud maturity model and the closer to Mode 2 you get, the more scripting becomes the only way to do work. If you and your team don't script today, it is vital you learn this skill. The best way to operate your Cloud is to apply an "everything-as-code" mindset. Development and infrastructure are converging. This becomes more obvious as you progress along the Cloud maturity model. Sharing code repositories from the developers with the infrastructure teams makes a lot of sense. Build a central repository, Azure DevOps is free for up to five users or you could use GitHub. Next, get team members to collaborate together to build out this repository. Your first scripts don't need to be fancy, but they should save you work.

For example, suppose you regularly refresh a test region with data from the production system before testing a release Script it. Having done this a few times, you may take the next step. You may realize you don't even need the test system most of the time. You could consider using a script to automate the provisioning of this test region. You have now saved both time and money. As you get better at scripting you draw closer to the next generation of automation and management: DevOps.

Chapter

DevOps and Application Development

Every company needs to be a software company

Satya Nadella (1967 –), Microsoft CEO

WE dissected in detail in Part 1 the wave of digital disruption that is sweeping the world at present. We looked at the opportunities and threats that this presents. Technology has phenomenal power to disintermediate and radically transform different industries. We introduced the concept that every company needs to be a software company. But what does this mean? How does a company become a software company? How do you place technology at the core of everything you do? Of course, there are a hundred answers to this question. In this chapter we tackle perhaps the most complex of them. How do you start to build a software development function within your business and within your overall Digital Operating Model? How do you put processes and governance around what is fundamentally a fast moving, fast changing and highly creative discipline?

> For further reading on innovation and becoming a software business, visit:
> *https://aka.ms/adopt/innovate*

What is DevOps?

This perhaps is one of the most difficult definitions within your Digital Operating Model. There are entire books, several times the size of this one, which inspect, dissect and attempt to define this nebulous word. Is it a set of tooling? Is it a process? Is it a redefinition of roles and responsibilities? Is it a change in corporate culture? The answer is, all of the above. It represents a paradigm shift in thinking about software engineering and operational management. A very simple definition is:

> The way to empower developers to produce high quality software, which solves real business challenges, and which can be automatically tested and deployed into a secure environment where end users can access it.

There are, of course, several orders of magnitude of complexity surrounding part of that definition, but as a concept it is simple. Developers write code. We need to test that code and we then need to deploy that code. Easy, right? Not quite so easy, no!

The great war

If DevOps is what we want, what are we replacing? Grab your sandals, it's time to go tree hugging.

If we look at the typical software development lifecycle today, one of the biggest challenges is that there are multiple disciplines at play. Developers write code. They understand code and object-oriented programming. They understand abstraction and parallelization, and the vast array of tools and techniques available to deliver the magic of software. Operations folk deploy code. They understand servers and switches and security. They understand load balancers and firewalls and all the components that software needs to live and run on.

Both are intrinsically important, and they are symbiotic. If business is from Mars and IT is from Venus, then developers are from the Milky Way, and operations are from another galaxy, far, far away. Not only are the two teams far removed intellectually, they are typically far removed geographically and organizationally as well. Very often, they report into two completely different parts of the business.

And so, the great war has raged, since the dawn of IT time. Developers sniping at operations. Operations sniping back at developers. These are two sets of individuals symbiotically linked, yet in a constant state of tension and warfare. Frankly, it's a miracle that anything at all gets deployed into production today in many organizations. When it does though, it typically takes weeks or months of waiting, testing, deploying, fixing, re-deploying, more waiting, more testing and so on and so on. Everybody is doing their job the way they are supposed to be doing it. The one set of people who suffer is the business.

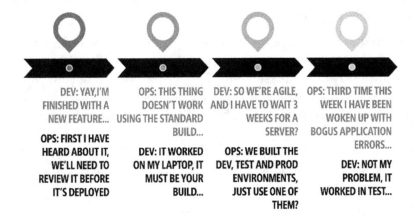

DEV: YAY, I'M FINISHED WITH A NEW FEATURE...

OPS: FIRST I HAVE HEARD ABOUT IT, WE'LL NEED TO REVIEW IT BEFORE IT'S DEPLOYED

OPS: THIS THING DOESN'T WORK USING THE STANDARD BUILD...

DEV: IT WORKED ON MY LAPTOP, IT MUST BE YOUR BUILD...

DEV: SO WE'RE AGILE, AND I HAVE TO WAIT 3 WEEKS FOR A SERVER?

OPS: WE BUILT THE DEV, TEST AND PROD ENVIRONMENTS, JUST USE ONE OF THEM?

OPS: THIRD TIME THIS WEEK I HAVE BEEN WOKEN UP WITH BOGUS APPLICATION ERRORS...

DEV: NOT MY PROBLEM, IT WORKED IN TEST...

Figure 25 - The DevOps problem statement © Servian

Restructuring your team

Developers and operations need to work seamlessly together in this new world. What does this mean to the way their teams are structured and how they collaborate?

The answer is, a lot. As we stated above, DevOps is not a thing in its own right. It is comprised of several initiatives and changes to the way people work. Most importantly, it requires a change of culture. There can be no more them and us. There can be no more division and conflict.

Patrick Debois, the father of DevOps, coined the term at his first conference. From then on organizations went about creating new silos of teams that would do both the dev and the ops, or somewhere in between and own the "pipeline" or delivery. This was precisely what Patrick was looking to avoid.

At the heart of the DevOps machine and culture movement is the quest to remove the number of handoffs between the teams and the organizational structures involved in a task. That applies whether it is a dev task or an operational one. Building a team that sat in between caused the problem to become worse. In more modern DevOps practices, we've learnt that team responsibility needs to remain with the team that is best qualified and skilled. So how is the DevOps team established? It's about lowering the walls between the teams and providing a high level of communication. This requires a common language. Teams still own their respective areas of responsibility, but all teams have the ability to make change in all other verticals.

The best practice example of this is that of the glorious "firewall change". The development team may well require a port changed. But they may not understand the implications of just opening up port 80 to the whole world from the database server. They ask the operations team to do it, and there follows the customary fight. The operational team would do better to allow the development team to see the infrastructure as code that wraps the security port protocols. That will allow the developer to "raise a pull request with the change".

This gives the operations team two things.

1. The opportunity to explain to the development team why just opening the port may not be a good idea. They can explain what else needs to be considered or changed.
2. The ability to protect against the developer just making the change and causing issues.

Likewise, the operational team may want to look at the developer's code or at least the process flow. Then they can see why they're trying to make a call on port 80. They can talk to the developer and suggest a different way to make the call. Either way, that communication is the new "DevOps Team" at work. Roles and responsibilities are respected, but hand-offs are reduced. If the port change was fine to make, the operations team would just click go and allow the roll out to occur – no questions asked.

There is no simpler practical step to achieve this than a realignment of reporting structure. Today, operations typically report into some kind of head of operations. Development reports into some kind of head of development. Often these reporting lines don't converge until you get into the upper echelons of an organization at some kind of directorial level. This doesn't work. Within a DevOps world, either developers need to report into operations, or operations need to report into development. Or better still, do not have operations and developers. Just have a software engineering organization that consists of folks with a slant towards development and folks with a slant towards deployment and management. Some organizations completely drop the term operations team and rename these people site reliability engineers. This demonstrates that their role is now all about making code work effectively and efficiently in production, and that they work hand in hand with developers.

There is another substantial change to understand and act upon. The roles of some of the people within each of these teams must change. Developers need to start thinking a bit more like operations folk. They should understand that they are not just writing code that will end up on some server somewhere – a server that they have no appreciation of or care for. They now know their code will end up within some form of Cloud service, probably chosen by either themselves or the architects within their team. They need to make sure their code is designed in such a way that it will seamlessly deploy into these services This requires that they respect some form of service-oriented or microservice-based architecture.

The bigger change is typically within the operations team. As we will explore below, there are the cultural changes and adaption of roles. But the biggest change is the tooling and automation that DevOps necessitates. IT pros have been doing automation and scripting for many years. In a DevOps world this takes on an ever-greater importance. It becomes the only way that anything can ever be done. No more manual steps. No more workarounds. No more provisioning environments. Everything needs to be automated. Everything becomes templated. This may prove a big challenge to some team members who are used to doing things their way. They are accustomed to drawing low level infrastructure design documents. Some folks may not make it. Others will embrace the new way of working and become excited about the power this level of automation can bring.

Automation and tooling

Good. You've fixed the culture. You've fixed the organizational structure. Everyone is behind this new world and this new Digital Operating Model. What's next? Tooling.

Those of you running a mature software development function will have some form of software development lifecycle management (SDLC) tooling. You may use TFS. You may use Jira. You may use several tools. They probably work quite well and help you manage requirements capture and source control. Those functions remain, and by and large will be unchanged in a DevOps landscape. What you need to add is continuous integration and continuous deployment (CI/CD).

There are, again, a vast variety of tools in this space It is possible you may use some of them already. Examples are: Azure Pipelines, Chef, Puppet, Ansible, Jenkins, TeamCity, and Octopus. There are more tools than you can shake a stick at. Each has strengths, and each has weaknesses. This book will not attempt to delve into the details of how you set up an end-to-end CI/CD pipeline. We will not discuss how you inject security and shift left thinking. Nor will we go into which tool makes most sense based on what technologies your developers use, and what technologies your operations team feel most comfortable supporting. That would require a book of its own. There are many books on the market you can refer to. We will only introduce you to some of the concepts. The important thing is for you to ask the smart questions about how you can introduce DevOps into your organization.

Ultimately though, you need to do the research and make this tooling the foundation of your Digital Operating Model. In a world of digital disruption and digital innovation your application development function becomes your powerhouse. Giving teams access to the best tooling is the best way to help them be effective and deliver the right outcomes for the business. Get it right and you'll truly be able to deliver the dream outcome: rapid, agile delivery of software to your users and customers.

If you want to skip a step, however, and just choose something that works quickly and simply out of the box, Azure DevOps is your answer. Rather than cobbling together multiple different tools, pick one integrated platform.

Immutability

From the Latin, *"immutabilis"*. Unchangeable.

In the introduction we called out a significant challenge. This is the difficulty of supporting change within a traditional ITOM. We made the point that change is difficult. Change is dangerous. Change is something to be avoided. When we go deeper though, we discover these statements hold true because of one thing. That one thing is called mutability.

You may have heard about mutable and immutable – maybe in a computer science class. It's a programming thing, right? Correct. But now it's an infrastructure thing as well. As infrastructure becomes programmable, so the concepts found in programming become more applicable.

We've all experienced or heard stories about bugs and defects that appear in production. These bugs weren't noticed or couldn't be reproduced in UAT. The environments look exactly the same, yet somehow there is some tiny difference that you just can't quite track down. There goes your weekend!

In today's Mode 1 world, we have mutable instances of infrastructure. They are ones we can mutate. Mutable is defined as: 'that may be changed; subject to change'. The most basic example of a mutation is patching. We don't rebuild a server from scratch each time a patch is released from an updated ISO which has the patch baked in. We patch in place. But every time we install a patch or deploy an updated version of an application that runs on that server, we introduce tiny variants. Now we have tiny differences between what may or may not have succeeded at an MSI installer or DLL packager level. Two servers which started out identical are no longer identical. If you update different configuration items stored on these machines enough times, bad config or defects can also creep in. Indeed, the vast majority of defects in production are due to bad config across environments.

Why do we act in this way if it's so prone to producing error? The answer is because anything else is prohibitively expensive and complex. Building a server, however automated it is, takes time. It requires people. It needs coordination and approval. Applications are typically deployed on to multiple servers, all of which need provisioning. Applications won't magically install themselves. Someone has to do it. When you reinstall something, it typically breaks – at least 90 percent of the time.

Well, that used to be the case. But it's not the case anymore. The central concept behind Cloud computing is infrastructure and application automation. This delivers us the ability to leverage immutable environments. They are also known as ephemeral environments. We can make use of Azure Resource Manager (ARM) templates and technologies such as Desired State Config (DSC) and Azure Deployment Manager. Additionally, we've seen the vast adoption of Hashicorp Terraform and the HCL language used to both drive and integrate with ARM templates to manage resources in a more programmatic fashion. With their help an automation specialist can describe exactly what an instance of an application looks like. It doesn't matter how many servers and/or services it is comprised of. The automation specialist can describe the components of the application and how each can scale up and down independently of the other components. They can also describe exactly how to deploy the application and the configuration itself onto these underlying IaaS and PaaS services. They no longer need to worry about patching (whether it's using IaaS or PaaS). At a moment's notice a completely new, ephemeral copy of the environment and application can be recreated from scratch. That's game changing. It's also organizationally changing.

We wrote earlier about the changes that need to be made within your teams. Immutability is the central concept driving many of these requirements for change. We no longer feed and water (that is: administer) environments. We now create new ones through scripting. The more automated we can make the deployment, the better we can test it. At the same time, the likelihood lessens of defects getting into production. That's why these new folks are typically called site reliability engineers. Their job is to stop defects getting into production.

However, I can't just take an application I have now and magically make it support this new world. Infrastructure automation is very similar to software automation and development. It takes time. It requires new concepts to be introduced into existing architectures. Concepts such as stateless operation and centralized configuration. When we talk about applications which can exist in this new world, we typically talk about Cloud-native applications. Almost invariably, these applications are immutable. Proper DevOps also requires immutable environments which can be automated and deployed on demand.

Containers

To alleviate some of the challenges with IaaS-based deployments, containers have emerged over recent years. They offer some significant advantages.

A container is a bit like a VM. But instead of containing an entire server operating system, it just contains the application files. Multiple containers can then run inside a VM which itself includes the underlying operating system. Scaling containers up and down is quick and simple compared to scaling entire VMs up and down. The industry standard container is Docker.

Containers by themselves are not especially helpful, though. In the same way as you need something like Azure to automate and marshal the creation and destruction of VMs, you need the same for containers. You need high availability and fail-over between the underlying VMs. You need orchestration.

There are several open source container orchestration solutions in market. They include DCOS and Docker Swarm. The newest entrant, and the one which has become the industry standard in the last 12 months, is Kubernetes (K8s). K8s originated from Google but is now widely adopted by the other two major Cloud vendors, Microsoft and Amazon. Even VMWare, once in danger of letting the Cloud world sail by, has gotten into its K8s groove. Google's multi-Cloud platform, Anthos, is also built on K8s.

One of the founding architects of K8s now works for Microsoft. Under his guidance Microsoft has bet big on the Azure Kubernetes Service (AKS). This fully managed platform service automates and orchestrates all the work involved in deploying and managing containers.

If you're more focused on .NET, you can also make use of the Azure Service Fabric. Service Fabric brings all the capabilities of platforms such as Kubernetes, but also has significant additional capabilities.

Platform services

Whilst many believe containers are the only way to design and build modern applications, this is not necessarily true. One of the major advantages of working with a Cloud platform such as Azure is the availability of platform services. These are typically referred to as PaaS.

PaaS is a very different beast from infrastructure services or containers. This is so even when you are leveraging immutability and automation. At a high level, PaaS services are a set of capabilities delivered by the underlying Cloud service which can be consumed as services rather than delivered from servers – that is servers you have to patch and maintain or containers you have to deploy and orchestrate. Rather than building an SQL server cluster, I can now consume SQL as a service. I simply pay for the storage and performance requirements I want.

Naturally there are pros and cons to any deployment method. The advantage of PaaS services is that users no longer need to maintain underlying servers or container orchestration platforms. The downside is users lose some of the control and customization which is possible when you're in control of the end-to-end stack. Most platform services are themselves delivered under the covers by containers. SQL Azure is built on Service Fabric. App Service deploys IIS instances inside containers on top of VMs. The platform service is, in effect, a container orchestration service for specific containers – one that is designed and managed by the Cloud vendor.

In a DevOps setting, PaaS services can have significant advantages. Provisioning PaaS services is exponentially more straightforward than automating the provisioning and configuration of VMs or containers programmatically. Users can instantiate a complete platform service with a handful of API calls. That is instead of a complex set of deployment scripts. This makes creating immutable environments much more straightforward. Users can create and tear down specific PaaS instances more easily than a set of VMs or containers which might support them.

Platform services can also be seamlessly scaled up and down based on performance metrics. How many transactions/messages/operations do I need to support per second/minute/hour? The pricing model also exactly reflects these performance-based characteristics. With a VM-centric view of the world I might not know if it was more CPU, RAM or disk performance which was required. You typically just scale all of them up.

One relatively new entrant into the PaaS space is Functions-As-A-Service (FaaS). FaaS is an additional abstraction on top of PaaS that allows you to deploy and execute individual lines or modules of code. The pricing model for FaaS is typically based on the number of times code executes, rather than the size of the execution environment (server or container). This model allows you to align demand and cost even more closely. It also allows you even greater ease of deployment. Within Azure, FaaS is delivered by Azure Functions.

The downside of PaaS is that you do leave yourselves open to some level of platform dependence. The dreaded lock-in. If you target a specific platform service on a specific Cloud, it can be more difficult to migrate to another Cloud vendor in the future. Whilst lock-in is typically overstated by the multi-Cloud zealots, it is nevertheless a real danger. Before you become too dependent on a given service, understand how you might theoretically migrate from one to another. For databases-as-a-service this might be as simple as a backup and restore. For event-based services, this might be a change of API call. If you want to use functions, choose a language that works across the FaaS offering of multiple Clouds (such as .NET Core). Don't use lock-in as a reason not to use platform services but be wise to what you're getting into and how, in theory, you might move if you needed to. In general, the ease of consuming these services easily outweighs any remediation work you might need to do in the theoretical scenario of having to move in the future.

One of the safest places to explore and take advantage of native FaaS services, like Azure Functions, is in the realm of operational glue. That is, where services need to manage an event and trigger another service or event, Azure Functions play a perfect role. For instance, suppose you wanted to instantiate a container that processes the vectors in an image dropped into Azure blob storage. You could produce an Azure Function that executes only when a new file is realized in a particular folder. That would lead to a call to the Azure Container Service to spin up a docker container and process the file for vectors. Finally, that information would be passed back to a file in another folder. This can be quite powerful when deploying a fully event-driven and automated micro and Azure service architecture.

There are hundreds of platform services on Azure for data, messaging, media, device management, identity, security, and much, much more. It's vital that you explore how PaaS services might benefit your developers. Find out how PaaS can streamline your application development workflow. Be bold. Mandate PaaS first.

Testing

Alongside immutability, a central tenet of DevOps is testing. Immutability exists to aid, amongst other things, effective testing.

A key concept to understand is a failure model. There are two kinds of failure model: a deterministic one and a non-deterministic one. They are, in laymen-speak, a failure you can discover through effective testing and one which you cannot. The more wildcards you can remove from the equation (such as mutable environments or physical hardware), the more unexpected failures you can eliminate. We want to exist, as much as is possible, within a deterministic realm. Then we can, at least in theory, remove all defects through effective, complete and automated testing.

Doing effective, complete and automated testing is no mean feat. We need to test a lot of stuff. We need to test code. We need to test logic. We need to test UIs. We need to test integrations. The primary reason for testing is to fix things. So, we need to engage developers, at every stage. We need to *shift left*.

> "The term "shift left" refers to a practice in software development in which teams focus on quality, work on problem prevention instead of detection, and begin testing earlier than ever before. The goal is to increase quality, shorten long test cycles, and reduce the possibility of unpleasant surprises at the end of the development cycle – or worse, in production. [28]

In a shift-left world, we need to increase the lines of communications across the teams. Particularly we need better communication between the automation specialists in ops and the developers. The shorter we can get the feedback, the more quickly we can spot the defects and get them fixed.

In the first way, there was one-way communication from devs to ops. In the second way, there is basic return of information from ops. Only in the third way can we truly shift-left. That is when

---

[28] *https://devops.com/devops-shift-left-avoid-failure/*

there is constant, automated and detailed communication between development and operations.

This might consist of immediate and interactive telemetry that a developer can access in development. It might be detailed stack trace information from an environment closer to production. It might be a Microsoft Teams notification that a build has failed. The communication can come in many forms. The easier it is for a developer to access this information, the quicker they can find the issue, and the quicker they can fix it.

The testing we introduce, therefore, needs to be as automated as possible. We need to make extensive use of unit tests which can be executed and run at build time. We need to use ephemeral environments, so that our end-to-end testing can run against exact replicas of what our environment will look like in production.

Figure 26 - The first, second and third way of communications

We need to knit testing deep into our software development and release cycle.

One of the reasons change has been dangerous in the past is because it can introduce unexpected behavior. Our testing must be as thorough and automated as it can be. Then we will only be exposed, by and large, to deterministic failures. This allows change to be introduced at a much faster rate, without introducing additional risk. This is the raison d'être of Mode 2, Cloud-native application development and delivery. It is key to your digital transformation. If you can be sure change isn't going to break something, you're building on solid foundations.

Pipelines

Pulling all these concepts together is the pipeline. A pipeline is the principal component of continuous integration and continuous deployment (CI/CD). It is a workflow – a set of instructions for the steps required to deploy an instance or a component of a given solution.

The first step is to take the source code from the version control repository. This code is then built according to the build scripts.

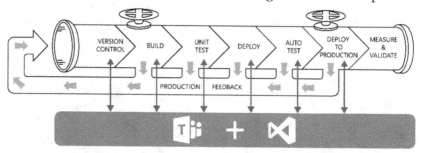

Figure 27 - A typical DevOps pipeline

Unit tests are then run within the compiled application and services. Once the tests pass, an instance of the application and/or services are deployed into an ephemeral environment. Further automated integration and acceptance tests are run before the environment is swapped/promoted into a production environment. Simple, right?

Unfortunately, not quite so simple! The pipeline is the magic that holds the whole DevOps world together. It's the asset that reduces hand-offs between teams. If your application is complex, your pipeline might end up incredibly complex and elaborate. You will typically have multiple pipelines for multiple applications or multiple tiers within an application. Depending on the tooling you use, your pipeline might need to speak to a plethora of separate tools and processes. Anyone who has been involved in automation knows that to automate a manual process is several orders of magnitude more complex than you might imagine. Things always find a way of going wrong.

But once you get your pipeline(s) working, it's something to celebrate. It's the magic that allows you to increase your rate of change exponentially. Do you need to change something? Just modify the code, check it in, press a button. Ta-da! It's in test. Press another button, and, ta-da! It's in production. When you can do this, you embrace change rather than fear it. You might not hit Amazon's million releases a year. But you might manage a release every week, or maybe even every day. That's huge progress for the vast majority of organizations.

Security

Security plays a very important part in this new DevOps world. Historically, security probably got involved reviewing low level designs. They may have asked for code drops to scan the source code. They probably enforced security software / patching schedules / penetration within production. It was a one-way conversation. Security would say in effect: We're going to tell you what to do, and once you comply, we will allow things to happen.

In this new world, security can become embedded into the process end-to-end. Policy is the key here. In the same way that we can express and enforce policy within our infrastructure deployments, we can now achieve the same within our application deployments. Rather than stipulating requirements up-front, such as encryption at rest, security folk can now access the same deployment scripts, templates and policies as developers. Security folk can modify these templates directly, enabling options and settings. When you leverage native compliance toolsets such as Azure Policy, these same controls can be enforced.

Security-related steps can also be inserted into the pipeline. The security movement within the DevOps methodology and mind-set has grown to such an extent that the term 'DevSecOps' has emerged. Entire groups of individuals are emerging just to tackle the automation that is security within the pipeline. Security used to be something designed at the beginning and validated at the end prior to the "go-live day". but we're now seeing organizations work to trust the pipeline over the end environments.

Automated code-scanning tools can check source code before it is built to look for vulnerabilities or bad code. If you're using containers, these containers can be scanned for viruses at the point they are created and sealed. You can then deploy as many instances of each container as you like, safe in the knowledge that each is virus free. You don't need to check your entire environment any more in production. You only need to check each of its building blocks at build time.

Monitoring

In the last chapter we explored some of the logging and monitoring tools available for your heritage estate. Depending on your application architecture, these tools also have applicability in this new world. We also have access to a range of other tools and services which are designed for a world of custom software engineering.

These tools capture additional metadata and telemetry which is not typically available to more infrastructure-focused tooling. Within Azure, Application Insights (part of Azure Monitor) provides rich data about the functioning of applications at the code, module, or container level. The following kinds of questions can be answered. How long does this call to the database take? What is the spin-up and spin down time of a container? What is the total number of individual transactions which make up my higher-level transactions? For instance, how many database calls are made per order? Having deep visibility into the functioning of your application is vital to ensuring its health. It also allows you to optimize its cost footprint.

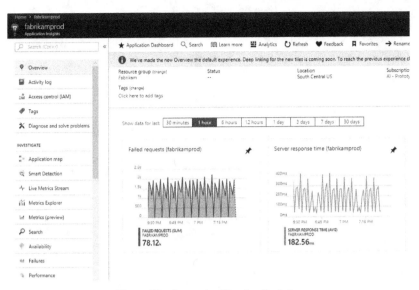

Figure 28 - Azure Application Insights

Chapter

14

The Technical Questions

Everyone hears only what he understands

Johann Wolfgang von Goethe (1749 - 1832), Writer

WE have outlined in this Part 2 of the book everything you need to think about as you start to build out your Digital Operating Model. As you have discovered, there is a lot to think about. Now we ask a second set of questions so that you can dig deeper. We want to position these challenges and decisions by means of questions in tabular format.

These questions are presented under the same headings as the preceding chapters (8–13) of Part 2 of this book. We pose 20 questions under each heading. If you need some context around the questions, turn back to the relevant chapter. This will remind you about the rationale of the question and will guide you towards the best answer.

You may not find the answer to every question. You might need to consult internally. You may need help from your vendors or from a partner. Don't panic. This is a complex subject and answering all of the questions will take time.

- **Chapter 8** – Strategy and Service Providers
- **Chapter 9** – Procurement and Financial Governance
- **Chapter 10** – Service Management
- **Chapter 11** – Access Control, Security and Policy
- **Chapter 12** – Monitoring, Management and Automation
- **Chapter 13** – DevOps and Application Development

14.1 Strategy and Service Providers

Getting your Cloud strategy right from the outset is the most important factor in determining the success or failure of your new Digital Operating Model.

In chapter 8 our headings are:

- Setting off in the right direction
- Cloud Center of Excellence
- Multi-Cloud
- Hybrid Cloud
- Your estate
- Bimodal IT
- Microsoft Cloud Adoption Framework for Azure - Define Strategy
- Service provider relationship
- Service level agreements
- Support

Some questions to ask about these topics follow in the table below.

☒	Question	Why this matters
☐	14.1.1 How much does the business think IT can be used as a key differentiator in the market?	We discussed in great detail in Part 1, the business part of this book, how IT can be used as a strategic differentiator. It's vital that the business accepts this as true. It's vital for them to accept the part you need to play in transforming the business.
☐	14.1.2 Has the business got clear and documented goals in the form of a business strategy with a 1–, 3–, and 5– year view?	This is a very important starting point. If the business is struggling to articulate what it needs to do to be successful, it is very difficult for IT to draw alongside and deliver meaningful change.
☐	14.1.3 What is the perception of the IT function within the business?	Part 1 examines this topic in more detail. The key here is that if IT is relegated to the role of keeping the lights on, it will take some effort to win hearts and minds. It will be hard for IT's role to be elevated to that of trusted advisor to the business.
☐	14.1.4 Has the business undertaken an exercise to align IT strategy with the business strategy?	This is where real traction starts to take place. The objective here is to map business objectives to IT objectives. The purpose is to ensure that the IT function is delivering the capability to the business in the way and at the pace they need for its success.

☒	Question	Why this matters
☐	14.1.5 Can the business articulate what IT delivery and transformation programs are aligned to which business goal? Does it know how the IT capability will contribute to the stated goal?	If the business has a strategy and the IT group has a strategy and they are aligned, you are in a good place. You will be able to deliver on the vision. However, the business stakeholders must understand this plan and buy in to its importance. It is good to have the plans; it is better if everyone keeps them front of mind and is engaged in actively using and adjusting them over time.
☐	14.1.6 If the answers to questions 14.1.4 and .5 are no, would the business be prepared to undertake a body of work to understand and document these objectives?	If none of this exists in your organization, it is important to get commitment to undertake some of this planning work. This is something you can do internally. Alternatively, there are external consultancies who can help with this important piece of work.
☐	14.1.7 Do senior IT stakeholders in the business see their role as a key contributor to the overall business success?	Unless and until IT leaders accept their importance to driving home the businesses strategic vision, they will remain relegated to a supporting role. If you don't have people in your IT team who accept this responsibility, get some new people.

☒	Question	Why this matters
☐	14.1.8 Is the business locked into a multi-year outsource? If so, what options are there to deliver services alongside this?	Traditional outsource contracts seek to avoid change and maintain the status quo. They are incompatible with a DOM. If you are currently outsourced, find out what you can do outside of this relationship. Start to gear the business up for the next renewal. At that time, you can insource again or engage a modern Cloud solutions provider.
☐	14.1.9 Does your organization use charge back for IT services or do IT hold all the IT budgets?	One of the major benefits of moving to a Cloud model is visibility into costs. You can cross-charge other departments for their IT. If these departments have not had to pay for their IT before, they may not see this as a welcome step!
☐	14.1.10 Do you have a vision for a multi-Cloud strategy?	Multi-Cloud sounds great. Why wouldn't you want it? In reality, it's orders of magnitude more complex than you might realize. Also, it doesn't necessarily deliver huge benefits. It's a decision not to be taken lightly.
☐	14.1.11 What is driving your decision to go multi-Cloud?	If you do want to go multi-Cloud, what is the driving factor behind this decision? Is it cost optimization? Is it avoiding lock-in? Is it to leverage capabilities unique to a specific Cloud platform? Sometimes there are valid reasons. If you really want to go multi-Cloud, make sure you can give clear explanations for wanting to do so. You'll need them later when you have to justify the huge additional complexity.
☐	14.1.12 If you do want to go multi-Cloud, can you hedge the complexity risk?	There are strategies that allow you to hedge against the additional risk and complexity of multi-Cloud. Choosing a development platform consistent across all container platforms can help. Kubernetes is a good example. Also consider the concept of general-purpose vs specialized Clouds.

☒	Question	Why this matters
☐	14.1.13 If you do want to go multi-Cloud can you leverage common tooling?	Monitoring and management are as important as deployment in a multi-Cloud world. Choose a solution such as Azure Log Analytics which works across different Clouds.
☐	14.1.14 Do you have legacy applications which might not move to the public Cloud?	There are several reasons why your applications might not move to the public Cloud. Your apps might run on legacy hardware such as mainframes or specialist machines. You might not be able to license your applications within a virtualized world. You may have a very low latency requirement between different tiers of an application. In these situations, you need to consider a hybrid Cloud strategy.
☐	14.1.15 Have you just made significant investments in replacement hardware?	There are reasons why organizations might have done this. Your hardware might have been so old and so unreliable that you had no choice. You might have been led to believe that a private Cloud was the same as a public Cloud. You might not have discovered Cloud early enough. In these circumstances, there can be challenges to adopting public Cloud. But in a hybrid world you might still be able to take advantages of some public Cloud capabilities.

☒	Question	Why this matters
☐	14.1.16 Are your requirements for data storage incompatible with public Cloud security?	Many organizations, especially public sector ones, have rules about what data can be stored where. Official and official sensitive data can be stored in the public Cloud, but secret data cannot. In this circumstance, hybrid can deliver some major advantages. You can construct a DOM which straddles public and on-premises Cloud. At the same time, dedicated hardware in a traditional datacenter will look after high-security requirements. Appliances such as Azure Stack can help here.
☐	14.1.17 Do you store large quantities of historical data?	Hybrid can play an important role here. Frequently accessed, hot data can remain on premises. Historical, infrequently accessed data can be moved to the public Cloud.
☐	14.1.18 Do you need a disaster recovery solution?	Hybrid can also play an important role here. Your primary environment will remain on-premises, but your fail-over, disaster recovery environment moves to the public Cloud.
☐	14.1.19 Do you run VMWare on premises today?	VMWare was the gold standard in days gone by. But it has failed to keep up with the industry's move to public Cloud. Its aborted attempt to get into this world with vCloud Air was mothballed. If you run VMWare on premises today, you will struggle to realize a true Cloud-native model. VMWare on Azure has just been released which will at least offer some hybrid capabilities.

☒	Question	Why this matters
☐	14.1.20 Are you a global organization with both centralized and regional deployments of workloads?	Work through your network connectivity plans before you start deploying workloads. You may end up with multiple hybrid data centers in region with global network connectivity. Microsoft has ExpressRoute premium which will allow you to use their global network instead of your traditional, expensive WAN provider.

14.2 Procurement and Financial Governance

This section corresponds to chapter 9 of the book. Once you've decided upon your Cloud strategy, you need to build processes around procuring it and governing it.

The way you procure Cloud services will be very different from the way you procured on-premises software. The organizations you procure it from will likely be different. The questions you ask of providers will almost certainly change.

The way you allocate and manage the cost of your new Cloud environment will change fundamentally. Charges will change from fixed up-front costs to variable ongoing costs. You could spend more than your thought. But you have the opportunity, with work and attention, to spend less than you thought. These challenges and opportunities need to be understood and managed.

☒	Question	Why this matters
☐	14.2.1 How does your business account for IT spend at the moment?	You may already have a sophisticated mechanism for understanding IT cost today, based on cost per user numbers and cost per line of business application. Alternatively, you may have a few big lines in your P&L and a lack of structure behind this.
☐	14.2.2 Can you state your IT costs per user or per application?	If you can't do this today, start to think about how you might represent this in your procurement and IT accounting costs. These will start to be the pillars you build on moving forwards.
☐	14.2.3 Do you normally wait until year end to bag the best deal from vendors?	Whilst the quarter end and year end pattern will never completely disappear from vendors, with a consumption-based model and an inability for the vendor to book revenue in line with orders, steep discounts to plug a gap in their numbers don't typically exist within a cloud world.
☐	14.2.4 Where do you buy your IT licenses and services from today?	Historically, most IT license spend was with IT resellers or License Service Providers (LSPs). In this new world, licenses can now be procured from a number of different people and styles of organizations. Cloud managed services businesses (MSPs) can bundles professional services and cloud consumption into one bill.

☒	Question	Why this matters
☐	14.2.5 Do you expect large discounts from vendors?	Whilst there are still some discounts associated with large commitments, typically for SaaS solutions, with IaaS and PaaS platforms, the margins are substantially lower and there is less opportunity for the vendor to offer these discounts. Instead, often vendors will leverage investment funds to pay for workloads to be moved to the cloud to drive increased usage and consumption.
☐	14.2.6 Have you chosen Microsoft as one of your strategic cloud partners?	Your procurement pipeline is an important asset to allow you to work with multiple cloud providers, you will typically have a different process to engage with your strategic partners. If you've already chosen Microsoft, don't let setting up a procurement pipeline for other vendors stop you getting to work with your strategic partners.
☐	14.2.7 Do you have a set of procurement questions that are fit for a cloud world?	Many traditional RFP sets of questions don't fit in this new world. You'll need to review them and work towards a new set that are fit for purpose. We have included a sample of the kinds of questions you might ask below.
☐	14.2.8 Where is your SaaS application delivered from?	Many SaaS vendors use a cloud deployment model themselves. If they use one of the major cloud providers, ideally one you use yourselves, you can forgo many of the detailed hosting questions you may have asked in the past as you will already know the answers to them.

☒	Question	Why this matters
☐	14.2.9 Do you use an IaaS or PaaS deployment model?	There is no right or wrong answer to this, but typically an IaaS deployment model may suggest a legacy application which has been "cloud washed". Vendors using PaaS will have needed to have done extensive re-architecting which demonstrates their real commitment to cloud.
☐	14.2.10 What is your shared responsibility model with your cloud provider?	Firstly, they should immediately understand this question. If they don't panic. Cloud vendors support SaaS vendors to some extent, depending on whether it's IaaS or PaaS. SaaS vendors should know intimately what they are responsible for and what the cloud vendor is responsible for and should have a documented RACI matrix for this.
☐	14.2.11 What is your high availability/ disaster recovery (HA/DR) plan?	A cloud deployment model doesn't magically give SaaS providers HA/DR out of the box. These concepts are as important in a cloud deployment model as an on premises one. Make sure your SaaS vendor has thought through all these challenges and has a good answer to them.
☐	14.2.12 What is your SLA?	When you move to a SaaS-based application you are going to be wholly reliant on the SLA of your SaaS provider. How does their SLA intersect with that of their hosting provider? Have they carefully thought through composite SLAs based on the range of cloud services their application hosting leverages?

☒	Question	Why this matters
☐	14.2.13 What technology stack do you use? What is your architecture?	Whilst less important due to the nature of SaaS delivery it's always interesting to know what technologies the SaaS provider uses. Do they use a traditional relational database or a schema-less NOSQL database? Do they use SOAP or REST service endpoints? All of these will give you clues about how serious and technically sophisticated the vendor is.
☐	14.2.14 Is your solution single tenanted or multi-tenanted?	Again, there is no right or wrong answer to this. Vendors might choose single-tenancy for compliance or performance reasons, alternatively they might choose it because they don't want to invest the time to re-architect for the cloud. Typically, a multi-tenanted design is better as it reduces the vendor's cost, which they can pass on to you, and it demonstrates it is actually SaaS software, not just on premises software "delivered through the cloud".
☐	14.2.15 What is your update frequency?	True SaaS vendors will operate on an "ever green" basis and make frequent changes to their code base. Those that only deliver updates every few months probably haven't fully embraced cloud / DevOps within their own organization.
☐	14.2.16 Does all IT spend need to go through procurement?	Traditionally, when there were large CAPEX spends behind infrastructure projects, this approach made sense. With smaller procurements from cloud vendors, this model can become prohibitively time consuming and expensive.

☒	Question	Why this matters
☐	14.2.17 How are IT budgets expressed and spent today?	With cloud deployment models, configuration changes or adding and removing users can have substantial and immediate effect on your usage charges. Budgets need to become much more flexible and capable of being "spent" without as much control and governance as you may have today. Techniques such as quotas rather than budgets can make more sense.
☐	14.2.18 Do you have the ability to apply budgets to departments or cost centers?	Much of the governance you will introduce to your cloud environment will be the enforcing of cost allocation. In order to enforce this allocation, you need to have the appropriate level of granularity within your existing cost code structure.
☐	14.2.19 Do you have approach levels of delegation within your budget and cost code structure?	By using cloud, you have fine grained control of who, at what level, can spend what. This is something you may consider within your budgeting and financial governance model. For example, a person in role x can increase spend by up to £x / hour, but someone lower down in the organization in position y can only increase costs by £y / hour. This allows a shift from an absolute to a relative definition of a budget.

☒	Question	Why this matters
☐	14.2.20 Who is now in charge of monitoring spend and introducing optimization?	No matter how hard you try and what controls you put in place, you will almost certainly end up spending more than you should. There will be things left on or licenses connected to people that don't need them. There will be servers deployed that are too big or not being used. There may be defects which drive increased consumption. As you move to the cloud, place someone in charge of cost optimization. Someone whose entire job revolves around asking all the annoying questions about why this is needed and why the specification of a given server is too high. Give them tools to help them do this programmatically and automatically.

14.3 Service Management

This section corresponds to chapter 10 of the book. Service management is at the core of your IT operating model. It governs just about everything related to how you consume and manage your IT services.

You almost certainly have a slick process today. But your service management realm will likely need extensive attention and change as you move into a Digital Operating Model.

ITIL has served us all well over the years, but the prescriptive processes in its current version may not be your bedrock into the future.

☒	Question	Why this matters
☐	14.3.1 Do you use ITIL today?	ITIL offers a lot of value to organizations today and has seen a substantial update with v4. But in previous incarnations, it can introduce additional complexity and processes which can severely reduce the effectiveness of your DOM rollout.
☐	14.3.2 Do you use SIAM today?	Service Integration and Management (SIAM) was a great concept in its time. It allowed large, monolithic and complex IT operating environments to be broken up into bite-sized chunks and distributed to different service organizations. The idea behind it is still valid, its current implementation is not hugely appropriate for a next generation DOM.
☐	14.3.3 Are you locked into a SIAM model?	You may well have contracted with a SIAM provider, or have SIAM constructs embedded within your existing operating model. If you do, it doesn't mean you can't introduce a DOM. But if you do, you will almost certainly have to free it from the bounds and controls that your other towers need to adhere to.
☐	14.3.4 Do you want to bring additional partners into a multi-source model?	For organizations that have been completely outsourced, bringing additional partners in can be challenging. Consider how you will manage these additional partners alongside your incumbent. You may need to introduce a role or team responsible for vendor management and integration.

☒	Question	Why this matters
☐	14.3.5 How will you manage integration between these partners?	Whenever you have multiple partners or vendors there are extra complexities around how these partners and vendors will work together. Ensure you spend the time to map out the interdependencies and the processes you will use to hand off between these people. This must be done in a controlled way.
☐	14.3.6 Are you able to break your IT service provision into a portfolio approach?	Portfolio is the more modern approach to IT service delivery. Rather than individual service lines, think about how these can be grouped-up into cross-tower functional capabilities which can be presented back into the business.
☐	14.3.7 Do you have a mature incident management process?	You do? Great. You typically won't need to make major changes to this. Incidents will still occur in the Cloud. You'll need to manage them. Some will be minor; some will be major. Understand how you will interface and get updates from the new players in your process. But for the most part we're talking evolution not revolution.
☐	14.3.8 Can you automate any of your incident management processes?	With a move to the Cloud there are growing opportunities to automate things. Incident management is a candidate ripe for automation. Can you automatically undertake remediation work to fix a known problem? Can you apply AI and machine learning to automatically make suggestions to support operators on things that they can try?

☒	Question	Why this matters
☐	14.3.9 Can you apply a new mindset in which you destroy and recreate rather than fix?	With increasing automation and standardization, there could be less need to *actually* fix things. In the same way you just throw away a broken TV and buy a new one, so will you be able to with aspects of your IT environment in the future. If a laptop is misbehaving, factory reset it and automatically rebuild it rather than trying to fix the problem. The same can be true for servers and application environments.
☐	14.3.10 How mature is your change management process?	Change management will be the process most profoundly impacted by a move to the Cloud. Change management is in the front line of the battle between agility and control. It is purposely designed to reduce risk which in turn means resisting change. Map out your change process and understand how you need to go about changing it (no pun intended!).
☐	14.3.11 Do you require all changes to go to a change advisory board (CAB)?	CABs generally serve two purposes. Firstly, to inform everyone about what is happening and secondly to allow people to speak up if they identify risk as part of a change. The first of these can now be achieved by other means, such as release notes and automated communication. The second should become less of an issue as change becomes the norm rather than the exception. Review what changes *really* need to go to a CAB and which can bypass it moving forwards. This assumes that appropriate controls, policies and guard rails are in place.
☐	14.3.12 How will you deal with authorizing new capabilities on the platform?	The evergreen nature of Cloud services means new features will appear continuously. You need to understand how you will deal with them and how you will release new capabilities to users.

☒	Question	Why this matters
☐	14.3.13 Do you have early adopters / champions internally?	Successful organizations select a cross section of their user population to act as a test bed for new capabilities. Do this before the capabilities are rolled out to the wider user group. In this model you can undertake proofs of concept and detailed testing.
☐	14.3.14 Do you have tiered support teams across each of your service lines?	As you move further up the Cloud IaaS > PaaS > SaaS stack, there will be a diminishing requirement for in-house second- and third-line support teams. The Cloud vendor will provide these. Think about how you can redeploy these capabilities internally for instance into automation teams.
☐	14.3.15 How will you interface with your Cloud vendor's support organization?	You may need support from your Cloud vendors, either in connection with service or configuration issues. You must understand who will deliver this support and how it will be delivered. Will you interface directly with the vendor? Or will you go via a reseller, or your Cloud managed services provider? Understand the roles and responsibilities in the chain and what you will need to do in the future.
☐	14.3.16 Do you have a Microsoft Premier Support Agreement?	You will need to consider which participants hold which support contracts for your DOM. If you are working with a Cloud managed service provider who has a Microsoft Premier contract and can make it available to you, do you need your own one moving forwards?

☒	Question	Why this matters
☐	14.3.17 How will you support internally developed applications?	As you move into a world of automation and DevOps your support organization will change profoundly. Issues impacting service will move from being predominantly infrastructure or configuration issues to being predominantly code and automation issues. Think about how your platform services and development teams will play a part in the support organization. 'It worked in test' will not cut it moving forwards. Developers and automation specialists would be wise to get ready for that call at 3am.
☐	14.3.18 Do you have shadow IT in place today outside your control?	You may already have applications and services which sit outside your service management realm. You need to consider how to bring them into this new service management structure.
☐	14.3.19 Do you have clear and measurable business and technology SLAs in place?	SLAs change radically as you move into this Cloud world. You need to understand how you can meet your existing SLAs. You must also manage the SLAs that come with the matrix of new suppliers and vendors that form part of yourDOM. You may consider introducing new measure and KPIs such as Net Promoter Score (NPS) to get a better understanding of the success and operation of your new DOM?
☐	14.3.20 Are you familiar with ULAs and VLAs?	User Level Agreements (ULAs) and Value Level Agreements (VLAs) are the direction of travel for the interface between business and IT. You need to understand them as concepts and build a path to deliver against these new metrics.

14.4 Access Control, Security and Policy

This section corresponds to chapter 11 of the book. Getting access to and securing your new Cloud environment is of paramount importance. Security used to be the big block to moving to the Cloud. That situation has now been reversed. Cloud vendors lead with the security of their offerings. Many organizations still do not appreciate that fact.

Using a secure Cloud platform is only half the solution. There's no point having a state-of-the-art security on your house or car if you leave them unlocked! Security in the Cloud is a shared model. The vendor is responsible for a great deal. But you'll also be responsible for a fair bit.

This challenge must be viewed through multiple lenses. Identity and access control are the things to think about. So too is physical and network security. Finally, you'll need to think about how you provide these capabilities to users and make sure your provisioning and JML processes are secure.

☒	Question	Why this matters
☐	14.4.1 Do you have a Chief Information Security Officer?	If you do, get them involved right now. Put the book down. Send them an e-mail. Tell them you want to meet as soon as possible to get them on board with what you are thinking. If you don't, you'll regret it later. They can be your greatest ally or fiercest opponent. Find out which as soon as you can.
☐	14.4.2 What is your CISO's approach to risk?	CISOs come from different backgrounds. Among them you will encounter fundamentally different approaches to risk. Some will be open-minded. Others will be set in their ways. If they love to look at low level infrastructure designs, you're going to need to help them see beyond these. The quicker you can identify how supportive they will be with your Cloud journey, the sooner you can find out how much time you need to set aside to get them on board. Without them, you're dead in the water.
☐	14.4.3 Does your organization have a documented set of security principles and rules?	If you do, this may be a good thing, or it may be a bad thing. If the security principles and rules run to hundreds of pages, you're in for a lot of work. But at least you have a strong foundation to build on. Get hold of the document and read it. Get a sense of how specific it is. In other words, determine to what extent it is related to traditional methods and models. It may just describe high level principles and rules. If it simply describes best practices, you're good to go as you can easily replicate these within a Cloud context. If it mandates things like VPNs and physical access tokens, you're going to need to get it changed, fast.

☒	Question	Why this matters
☐	14.4.4 Do you use Active Directory on premises today?	Your Cloud identity model, typically, is built directly from your on-premises Active Directory environment.
☐	14.4.5 What state is your Active Directory in today?	Moving to a Cloud identity model means your on-premises environment must be in good shape. There are things that you might have gotten away with on premises. They include duplicate namespaces and accounts with rogue characters. This kind of thing won't cut the mustard in the Cloud. You may have acquired other organizations and bolted their ADs onto yours. Before you do anything, get your existing environment checked over. Get a report on how it looks and what you need to do.
☐	14.4.6 Do you use physical access tokens today?	Physical access tokens were great. They served a purpose in their time. With the Cloud, there are newer and better technologies to use, such as Azure MFA. These technologies are much more cost effective. They allow additional forms of authentication, such as phone calls, text messages and mobile apps. They can even stretch to the physical proximity of the phone to the laptop or to a geo location.
☐	14.4.7 Do you have an on-premises single sign-on solution in place?	You may leverage Active Directory Federation Services (ADFS) to provide single sign-on to users. If you do, you will probably have several connections you set up manually, exchanging certificates and keys. It probably works OK most of the time. You can probably keep this in place for some things. But in time you'll probably want to migrate it to something a bit more up-to-date such as Azure Active Directory.

☒	Question	Why this matters
☐	14.4.8 Do you have a Cloud-based single sign-on solution?	There are Cloud-based single sign-on solutions in market. Okta is one of the best known. These solutions do a great job and if you use one you will already be experiencing many of the benefits of moving to a new Cloud IdP. But if you do have these solutions in place, find out about the capabilities available natively on Azure, such as Azure Active Directory. You may not need these third-party solutions moving forwards.
☐	14.4.9 How are licenses impacted for JML in a Cloud world?	JML in a Cloud world is very different from how it is in the on-premises world. Providing access and revoking access to Cloud-based services starts and stops cost being accrued in near real time. It also requires licenses to be available in near real time. If you're on an EA, ensure you have sufficient headroom to support bringing users online quickly. If you are on CSP you must fully understand the mechanism to get additional licenses.
☐	14.4.10 How does security change for JML in a Cloud world?	Single sign-on is great. But it does mean users have access to a great deal of data and different services wherever they are. You need to ensure that your JML process is quick enough. You must be able to switch off access to these third-party systems quickly as employees change roles or leave the organization.
☐	14.4.11 What security solution do you use on premises?	You probably use one of the big brand security solutions on premises today, such as Check Point, F5 or Barracuda. Understand what the vendor's approach is to public Cloud. Do they support it? What is their licensing and deployment model?

☒	Question	Why this matters
☐	14.4.12 Do you require dedicated connectivity to your on-premises environment?	The answer to this is almost certainly yes. So, you need to understand what options are available from your telecoms provider. Do they support ExpressRoute? Which flavor? Who supports what?
☐	14.4.13 Do you want to route all your Cloud traffic, including internet breakout, on premises?	The immediate answer to this is often yes. And "yes" is sometimes OK. But understand the implications of this from a cost and performance perspective. Does everything have to transit via this route, or can you separate out some traffic, such as Microsoft Updates?
☐	14.4.14 Do you need to inspect and control the ingress and egress of traffic to the Cloud?	Azure and ExpressRoute have very sophisticated controls for data routing, and access control. But they have limited capabilities for traffic inspection. You may need to consider additional security products and services to inspect this traffic.
☐	14.4.15 What are your policies today on internal network security?	There are many approaches today to segregate traffic within internal networks, including VLANs. Understand how these map to the Cloud. Moving to the Cloud can also be a good excuse to ramp up your internal network security controls as they manifest within the Cloud. It's much simpler now to enforce stricter access control rules between network segments or require additional controls such as IPSEC.
☐	14.4.16 Do you use host-based firewalls and other controls?	If you don't use these on premises today, explore whether you can introduce them as part of your move to the Cloud. Best practice now is to have as much security within your networks as is enforced between and into your networks.

☒	Question	Why this matters
☐	14.4.17 Do you employ a service catalogue today?	Carefully consider how a traditional service catalogue fits into your newDOM. A service catalogue can be useful for some aspects of provisioning. In other ways it can be constricting.
☐	14.4.18 Can you embrace the notion of Cloud environments?	A Cloud environment can be a more useful construct to dovetail into a service catalogue. It allows users to serve themselves through your own service portal. But they can still use the native capabilities, such as the Azure Portal and APIs, to provision individual capabilities and services.
☐	14.4.19 What information would you need to collect from your users at the point of provisioning a Cloud environment?	There is a lot of information you could collect from users as part of a provisioning process. Try to balance the need for comprehensive reporting with making the process easy and streamlined.
☐	14.4.20 Do you have a requirement to span policy across multiple Clouds or provide additional reporting on compliance?	Azure Policy is specific to Azure. It is also policed by Azure. Some organizations may want to enforce policies across multiple Clouds. Or they might want to provide a separate, independent view of their compliance. Third party tools can provide additional capabilities in this space. Examples include: Palo Alto Evident, NeuVector and DivvyCloud.

14.5 Monitoring, Management and Automation

Monitoring, management and automation are at the heart of your Digital Operating Model. In chapter 12 we focused on managing your estate, as it looks today, in the Cloud. Azure provides capabilities to assist with automating your heritage workloads as you go through a process to make them more Cloud-native.

We described this model as a Gartner Mode 1.5. That is somewhere between a legacy, on- premises environment (Mode 1) and a brand new, Cloud-native Mode 2.

Moving to a more modern approach to monitoring and managing heritage workloads can have a big impact on your ITOM. It will almost certainly require migrating to Cloud-native tooling. That can be a major undertaking.

With these questions we'll hopefully help you to understand this first stage of your transition to becoming Cloud-native.

☒	Question	Why this matters
☐	14.5.1 What tool do you use for monitoring and managing your environment today?	There will probably be only a handful of people expert on your monitoring and management operating model. It's probably something that's been there forever. It just sits in the background doing its thing. Find out who's your expert and do some research.
☐	14.5.2 Do you have one, or a number of different tools?	You may have tried migrating tools in the past. You may have a mix of different tools, doing different things, supplied by different vendors. Your tool for monitoring patches may be different from your tool for monitoring desktops. Understand the entire landscape of your toolchain. Ideally draw it up into a diagram, if you don't have one already.
☐	14.5.3 Do you use System Center?	If you do, great. Your job will be easier. If you don't it's not a massive problem. You will probably need to migrate to new tooling anyway. You may just have a bit more work to do.
☐	14.5.4 Is your current monitoring system designed for an on-premises world?	Many of the tools in market today (including System Center) were built in the days of on premises. The clue lies in the name of some of them – names such as LanGuard. These tools naturally continue to evolve and support more Cloud workloads. But it's often very difficult to use these tools to support your new Cloud-native monitoring and your management operating model.
☐	14.5.5 What tool do you use for backup today?	In the same way that monitoring, and management tools were designed for the on-premises world, so too were backup solutions. You need to consider whether your solution is still valid in a Cloud world. Could you leverage Cloud-native tooling? You may be able to utilize a hybrid, where your existing solution hands off long-term storage to the Cloud.

☒	Question	Why this matters
☐	14.5.6 How do you do server patching today?	In a server world, the process is largely similar. But now you can make greater use of automation to power the end-to-end patch cycle across complex architectures. Azure can also automatically patch IaaS machines if you enable this
☐	14.5.7 How do you do device patching today?	In the device world, with modern management, clients now generally take their updates directly from Microsoft, governed by Intune. Most users have these updates forced on them as part of the evergreen Windows as a Service.
☐	14.5.8 Are your devices primarily on site or remote?	With modern device management, devices become Cloud-enrolled rather than on-premises. This can have advantages, such as better support for remote working. But it can have disadvantages, such as the additional complexity of managing a large number of office-based devices. Carefully plan your hybrid device management solution.
☐	14.5.9 How complex is your AD GPO structure?	In this new world of modern device management, Intune and MDM replace Active Directory and GPOs. Depending on the complexity of the policies you enforce today, there could be substantial work involved in migrating policies to MDM.
☐	14.5.10 Which edition of Windows 10 do you use today?	Many of the advanced, modern management capabilities are only available in Enterprise. You may need to reconsider your licensing strategy for devices. Enterprise is now available under the CSP licensing program (it used to be just EA).
☐	14.5.11 How do you use gold images to deploy OSs to devices?	With modern management, gold images are typically no longer required. Devices connect straight to Azure AD from the OOB experience. They immediately come under device control, are hardened and have applications deployed to them.

☒	Question	Why this matters
☐	14.5.12 How comfortable are you with Cloud domain-joining your devices?	With a move away from traditional Active Directory to Azure Active, management and security of those devices is now delivered exclusively from the Cloud.
☐	14.5.13 Are you aware of the release and support cadence for Windows 10?	There are two versions of Windows 10 – semi-annual and long-term service branch. Microsoft are encouraging users onto the semi-annual branch. The support model now dictates the September release will have support for 30 months and the March release will have support for 18 months. Consider how you will deal with this rapid update cycle to the underlying operating system.
☐	14.5.14 How do you install applications on devices today?	Automatic deployment of software installation packages is commonplace. The deployment is done via GPO and/or platforms like System Center Configuration Manager (SCCM). With modern management, these packages are deployed from the Cloud. You need to consider the amount of work involved in changing your application deployment methodology.
☐	14.5.15 What anti-virus software do you use today?	Most of the AV providers have embraced a Cloud world and their solutions play nicely with the Cloud. Some others do not. The capabilities of Windows Defender have also improved a lot over the past few years, which may negate the need for third party solutions.

☒	Question	Why this matters
☐	14.5.16 Do you envisage substantial portions of your server infrastructure remaining on premises?	This is an important design point and has implications for the design of your monitoring and management solution. If the majority of your estate will live in the Cloud in the near future, it may be appropriate to use Cloud-native technology alone, such as Azure Log Analytics. If lots of on-premises equipment will remain, you may need to keep System Center or an equivalent alongside it, at least for now.
☐	14.5.17 How much automation do you do today?	There are a lot of things you can automate on premises, especially when combined with virtualization technologies. If you're doing this today, great. You'll be doing a whole heap more of it in the Cloud. You will have the ability to automate things that you can't do on premises today.
☐	14.5.18 What is your team's level of skill with PowerShell?	PowerShell is the scripting language of choice within the Microsoft Cloud. If your team are not already whizzes on it, they need to become whizzes. Fast. Consider how you can support your team to upskill on this technology.
☐	14.5.19 How do you respond to alerts today?	Alert management is difficult. How do you filter the noise of warnings and spot the critical incident that needs to be fixed? This is one area where the Cloud can assist with machine learning, spotting the trends and finding that needle in the haystack.
☐	14.5.20 To what extent can you take corrective actions in relation to an alert?	If there are things you commonly have to do to fix an application that is malfunctioning, such as forcing a config update, can you automate this? Tools such as Azure Automation can be programmed with complex logic about what to do in different situations, and what to do to fix a problem.

14.6 DevOps and Application Development

Restructuring your organization to take advantage of DevOps is one of the most challenging aspects of taking on a Digital Operating Model.

It will have the biggest impact on your organizational structure of any of the changes you need to make. It will also be the set of changes which helps you best deliver and execute your Digital Operating Model.

If every business needs to become a software business, then every business really needs to build a DevOps culture and team within their organization.

☒	Question	Why this matters
☐	14.6.1 Do you have an internal development function?	If you don't currently develop software, this can be an advantage as you won't have an existing team to morph.
☐	14.6.2 Do you want an internal development function?	If you don't currently develop software, the question "do you *want* to" is a very important one. Getting into software development is not something to be done lightly. But it is becoming more necessary in order to digitally differentiate yourself.
☐	14.6.3 Do you have a software development lifecycle management (SDLC) tool in place?	Most organizations that do development today, will have an SDLC in place. You might use Team Foundation Server or the Atlassian stack. You will need to make much use of this SDLC tool as part of your DevOps initiative. Make sure you have one that properly supports it.
☐	14.6.4 Do you have preferences for a software development language and frameworks?	There is no right answer to this question. With Microsoft's Cloud there is no preference for one language or framework over another. .NET is the typical framework used by Microsoft shops, but it doesn't have to be: Java, Node, Go, Ruby or any other framework work seamlessly. If you have no preference, look to the availability and cost of resources to determine your best choice.
☐	14.6.5 Do you have an established operations team supporting your developers?	If you do, you may need to fundamentally rethink how they work alongside your developers. The role of the operations team will need to change. Start by evaluating their skill sets and their level of competency in scripting and automation.

☒	Question	Why this matters
☐	14.6.6 Do your development and operations reporting lines converge?	It's vital that development and operations report to the same person. This is the only way to truly embrace DevOps. If they don't, collapse the teams and put one leader in charge of both teams.
☐	14.6.7 Can you sustain rapid code releases?	Along with changes to roles, the biggest change in adopting DevOps is enabling rapid change. You need to understand if your codebase can support this.
☐	14.6.8 Do you have a modular architecture?	If you want to create an environment of rapid change and your current application(s) have a monolithic architecture, you may want to consider re-architecting them.
☐	14.6.9 Do you have centralized configuration management?	Most software defects can be traced back to configuration management issues. If you don't have centralized configuration management, you need it.
☐	14.6.10 How do you manage environments today?	In a world of DevOps, the traditional notion of environments fades away. With ephemeral environments, you can have as many or as few environments as you want. Consider how many environments you need and how you can support them.
☐	14.6.11 Do you utilize third party components or libraries?	In a world of automated deployment, you need to consider how easy it is to bundle and deploy third party libraries. You also need to understand any licensing implications of having more environments than you might have used previously.
☐	14.6.12 Is your application based on third party platforms?	If your application is hosted inside another platform, such as SharePoint or Sitecore, you will need to research how to support automated deployment in this model.

☒	Question	Why this matters
☐	14.6.13 Have you investigated containers?	Containers are the cool kids on the block right now. There can be benefits from containerization, but there are also some drawbacks. Additional platforms will be required to orchestrate containers.
☐	14.6.14 Can you leverage platform services?	Wherever possible, look to leverage PaaS components as part of your application architecture. This makes deployments easier and maintenance more straightforward.
☐	14.6.15 What delivery platform do you want to use?	There are many models for building and deploying code today. You might choose PaaS, containers, functions or something else. Make the choice carefully as it will have a profound impact.
☐	14.6.16 To what extent are you prepared to accept lock-in?	It's easy to say you are not in any way prepared to accept lock-in. But understand the ramifications of this statement. Some lock-in is sometimes OK if it can reduce development effort. Likewise, if you assess the cost of reversing out of an environment to be less than the cost of making it work within a different Cloud in the future it's an easy choice to make.
☐	14.6.17 Do you have availability requirements beyond that supplied by Azure?	Most applications can function within the SLAs offered by Microsoft. This is so long as the correct design patterns are adhered to and you utilize multiple datacenters. Some applications simply must never be allowed to go down. In this circumstance, you might want to investigate hosting across different Cloud providers.

☒	Question	Why this matters
☐	14.6.18 What is your approach to testing?	One of the prerequisites for DevOps is automated testing. It's the safety net that allows rapid deployments. If you don't currently have unit tests, you need to investigate the feasibility of introducing them.
☐	14.6.19 Can you automate your UI testing?	Testing code is great. To really rest safe in the knowledge that changes are not breaking things, you must implement UI testing.
☐	14.6.20 Can you automate integration testing?	Along with testing the UI, also consider how you can automate the end-to-end testing of your solution in place. You may need to create testing (mocked) end points to help with this.

Chapter

Funny You Should Say That

Laughter gives us distance. It allows us to step back from an event, deal with it and then move on.

Bob Newhart (1929 -), Comedian

FOR many organizations a credible Digital Operating Model cannot come soon enough. It is the missing piece for organizations with increasing (and in some cases total) reliance on Cloud services. They need to develop an organizational culture that has the business teams and IT team working in harmony. It will also help those organizations that have dipped their toes in the Cloud and then thought: What are we getting into? If you have yet to start your journey in the Cloud then: What have you been waiting for?

Notice the yellow sticky on the book cover with the three words: Secure. Compliant. Agile.

- **Secure**: We tell you all the capabilities to switch on in order to secure your environment
- **Compliant**: Ensure your IT environment meets your governance and policy requirements (e.g. for data encryption and data residency)
- **Agile**: This is the crux of the book. It has to do with how you deliver *agility* to the business team and control for the IT team. It is the IT team that has day-to-day responsibility for this strategic resource.

The best person to ask for advice is someone with experience. Find someone who has climbed the mountain, not just looked at the pictures, thinking: One day, maybe. There now follow two case-studies from people who have the experience. They chose to climb the mountain rather than look at the pictures.

If you have your own story, then we encourage you to share it at *stories@smart-questions.com*

John Kendrick

Cloud Transformation Lead, International Oil Company

Moving to "Cloud" was (and I should say still is) an emotional and challenging journey. The classic PPT (People Process Tools) activity goes into overdrive… Do not underestimate the impact, effort and how long this will take! That said, the benefits are huge.

Classic infrastructure generally takes weeks or months to setup kit in data centers with many teams involved. It's expensive and slow… and often processes used have been in place for many, many years.

The Cloud proposition is significantly better … but the disruption it brings is significant too! Creating vanilla infrastructure in the Cloud takes tens of minutes, but, all the hardening processes, port opening, active directory setup, everything that exist around it is from a time when infrastructure took weeks and months to get setup, and generally geared to have an SLAs (Service Level Agreements) that is setup to respond within in days (if not weeks); the SLAs are just not ready, and because of this, nor are the people.

When I embarked on it, we didn't realize quite how much disruption we would cause. We spent a long time doing what we could to automate as much as we could within our new processes. Automation of process within your own control should be non-negotiable – anything that involves your new Cloud platform must be automated as much as possible – remember, this is Infrastructure as Code, so treat it like that. However, no matter how fast you go, no matter how much automation you bring through your new Cloud construct, you can't get away from the fact that there are significant changes needed to "external" teams and processes. Assuming your company follows it, ITIL v3 will need to be interpreted in a very different light to ensure its alignment to the speed of Cloud.

Even when you battle through and as you begin to change the people, process and technology, you encounter the next challenge – the operating model. There are two elements to this. One, having a customer focus is really core – you need to create a service people want to use. Amazon and Microsoft have different technology offers, but they do have a very common theme of making it something that the customer wants and desires. The second is ensuring you are ready to have a service that can keep pace with the new Cloud offer – and very importantly be able to "resell" it within your organization. When we started on the Cloud journey Microsoft were just introducing ARM (moving away from Classic) and Amazon were churning out pretty significant improvements on their core products on a daily basis. We had to create an operating model that could leverage these new features, and to do this we developed a "product" based model, rather than a "project" based model to support the Cloud offers. The most significant challenge in this area was the release schedule – we were releasing improvements to enterprise Cloud infrastructure every two weeks; this was across both Amazon and Azure. A lot of people saw this as a huge risk – but it was actually essential… in fact, if we didn't keep pace, there was a higher risk if we stayed on older version of the various product offers.

Cloud offers amazing capabilities and with it HUGE (and I really do mean big) positive disruption. This isn't throwing a pebble into a pond and watching the ripples move out. This is almost akin to throwing a boulder so large in that it dislodges all of the water! Metaphorically the new ways of working are the water in which you will refill.

It's a brilliant move. One I fully advocate, and, had I known what I know now back when I embarked on the journey all those months ago, I probably would have been more nervous about my chance of success. That said, I don't think I would have changed anything with my approach – "do something, learn, do again, learn again, etc.". It was tough, it was hard work, but I was successful, and Cloud can (and if done properly will) be a positive impact on your company.

Pete Gatt

CEO, Vibrato & Partner, Servian

I'd love to tell a story about RLB in Melbourne, Australia. With a corporate history stretching back to the Industrial Revolution in the United Kingdom, Rider Levett Bucknall are market leaders in costs and project management for major building developments, including quantity surveying and advisory services.

RLB wanted efficiency in building and maintaining lots of environments...

Just liked described in chapter 13, the RLB team were operating with a small infrastructure team who whilst familiar with modern services within Azure to assist with automating their pipelines, weren't ready for production hand over. This is a tale that talks to the flow of developers and application specialists flowing into the platform services team, working with a partner and then flowing back into the application team, allowing Azure to maintain the platform management with minimal human and manual interaction.

As part of its core business, Rider Levett Bucknall (RLB) enables surveyors and project managers to operate efficiently on landmark building projects such as the Sydney Opera House and the 2012 London Olympics. This requires access to a scalable and robust data platform which is easily consumable.

When we got to RLB, we found that they had been working with US-based data specialists to develop a data platform completely customized to support its business workflows. This data platform was built and deployed in Microsoft Azure, and required a highly scalable, geo-redundant architecture to ensure that the custom solution could be accessed reliably, could scale rapidly to meet increasing demand, and could be quickly deployed into multiple global regions. Whilst the application was highly sophisticated, the platform and automation of environment creation and management wasn't in place. The teams had amazing developers and at the time, only a small team who were new to Azure and new to looking after these workloads. But this meant that building environments and deploying to environments was looking like days or weeks at a time for them. We (Vibrato, now Servian) thought, there's got to be a way we can continue to ensure they keep it simple and don't require a massive amount of engineering and continued engineer to look after this platform. So, we established a virtual platform services team in partnership with RLB and built on a foundation of Microsoft Azure Container Services, leveraging Kubernetes for container orchestration. There's more to the story and process, but the solution has enabled RLB to deploy changes from code commit into production across regions in minutes, whilst providing a unified environment for internal development teams.

We must scale this beast... globally...

The solution that we architected needed to adhere to certain critical business requirements, including database scalability and redundancy, automated deployment to Dev/Test environments and integrated approval gateways for production deployments. The development teams did not want to have to keep spinning things up differently in each region and didn't want to have to redeploy things manually each time... nor did we. We realized that if we're going to scale it, we're going to scale it in tiers. The solution was architected and delivered in three discrete components – an application tier built on Azure Container Services, a data tier leveraging Microsoft Azure SQL and an automated CI/CD stack founded on Microsoft DevOps. Working with RLB's development team which drove the internal adoption and development of application containers, Vibrato architected a fully automated solution which was redundant across multiple Azure regions with the capability to easily expand to any region globally.

The container-driven application tier was architected using Kubernetes for container orchestration, allowing RLB to define its entire application stack as source-controlled templates and maintain a unified deployment pattern across every environment and every Azure region.

So, about this CI/CD and DevOps Stuff...

To ensure that we minimized the requirement for people managed servers or services, we needed to ensure that every phase of the solution was delivered with strict adherence to the principles of Continuous Delivery, leveraging the native capabilities of Microsoft Azure DevOps (AZDO). Using Builds triggered from code committed to both GitHub and AZDO Git repositories, RLB was able to build and store custom application containers in Azure

Container Registry instances, then launching Releases with the same image across Development, Staging and Production environments. We had given the developers a simple way to leverage event driven builds through their SDLC seamlessly.

Kubernetes was used heavily for container orchestration, ensuring not only that the same image could be dynamically configured for each deployment environment, but that each service was self-healing and could be updated during business hours without end-user impact. Kubernetes was also used in combination with Microsoft Azure Traffic Manager to dynamically route users to the region with the lowest latency, whilst also providing secure communications and dynamic edge routing.

The native capability of AZDO to integrate with open source platforms such as Docker and Kubernetes ensured that RLB was able to build upon a single unified platform for Continuous Integration and Continuous Deployment, whilst maintaining the flexibility to deploy from a mixed pool of Windows and Linux agents.

Remember the part where they didn't want to have to maintain environments, this well and truly solved that and the Platform Services capability was handed to development teams to continue using not just for this service, but for the other services to come.

Deploying in minutes to production...

RLB's business and development teams were extremely happy with the solution, in particular the cross-region robustness and redundancy and the fully automated AZDO Build and Release pipelines. The abstracted, templated nature of the solution means that RLB's development teams were freed from ongoing infrastructure maintenance and can focus entirely on supporting the application and supporting the business by driving further innovation.

The adoption of container services and adherence to DevOps principles has enabled RLB to deploy application updates from code into production in mere minutes, whilst using the native capabilities of AZDO to maintain tight control over the end-to-end process.

And thus, RLB is now able to drive innovation and expansion, confident in the underlying technical foundations, giving the power back to the developer and letting the Azure platform take care of the rest.

So, what did we learn?...

- The harmonic operating model does not need to be fixed in place once established. In fact, Servian has since found that it's often better to establish and destroy platform service squads when paying off a NTOP TAX (new technology or process tax) rather than keep a team in place for good. In drives the ability for teams to not get fat and lazy and ensure they hand back solid IP, automation and process back to the development squads.
- It's possible to get your deployment down from weeks to minutes ... even to prod when using Azure DevOps in a highly integrated fashion.
- Kubernetes for the win! Allowing Azure to manage the clusters without breaking the back is far cheaper than building out an operations team.
- Models that hand the control back to the developer are good models. Developers are the Rockstars, we're just the Roadies in the background ensuring they put on an amazing performance for their fans.

Chapter 16

Final Word

A conclusion is the place where you got tired of thinking.

Albert Bloch (1882 - 1961), American Artist

FOR the business audience, we live in interesting times. This book was inspired by conversations with Microsoft and Microsoft customers and partners who had reached a point of no return along their Cloud journey. The evidence was for them compelling: Cloud is the future; it is where innovation lives; it rocks!

This in turn raised important questions: What does that mean for the existing IT estate? How should we deal with the rapidly increasing adoption of Cloud with a likely end state of being 'all in' on the Cloud? Some businesses are already committed to being 'all in'. Others are starting out, and for them unchartered waters lie ahead.

Part 1 of this book dealt with the conversations that surface as a business grows its dependency on the Cloud. It presents the argument for a Digital Operating Model. We broke that term down into the language of the business team and IT team. The Digital Operating Model is a discussion between the business teams and IT team wanting a 'let's make this happen' approach instead of 'locking horns'.

Perhaps we will look back one day and ask: What was all the fuss about? For now, there is an urgent need for practicality, and we hope this book offers that practical guidance.

F OR the technical readers; we've covered a phenomenal amount of ground together in Part 2 of the book.

We have delivered a soup-to-nuts journey from strategizing, through buying, managing, securing, monitoring and developing your new Digital Operating Model.

If you want one thing to remember from this whole discussion around agility and control, it's automation and code. Full, extensive and comprehensive automation is the secret sauce. It's what will allow you to discover that enigma that has escaped us for so long.

Your journey has just begun though. Getting from the theory in this book to the practice inside your organization is no mean feat. Depending on the size of your business, it might take anywhere from months to years. You may have decades of legacy you need to remodel and adapt. The journey will be fraught with challenges, both political and practical. You may have to crack a few eggs. You may have to bring a few new people in and let a few people go.

This is something you will almost certainly need help with. Reach out. Speak to others who have done it before. Seek guidance, counsel and help. Get in experts who have helped other organizations and can assist in avoiding the potholes and blind alleys.

Please do not be put off though. If you can pull through and deliver your new Digital Operating Model, you will be setting your organization up to succeed not only now, but for the next decade. You will deliver on what was only a dream up to now, combining agility and control. This will put technology at the core of what your organization does. It will transform you into a truly digital business.

We finish up with just two words.

Good luck!

Glossary

Agile

Agile is a methodology for modeling and documenting software systems based on best practices. It is a collection of values and principles, that can be applied on an (agile) software development project. This methodology is more flexible than traditional modeling methods, making it a better fit in a fast-changing environment. See Chapter 5.

agile

Small 'a' is used to describe an organization's intention to establish an agile culture for the collaboration of teams working to achieve a common goal.

Artificial Intelligence (AI)

AI is hot technology. It is the development of computer systems able to perform tasks normally requiring human intelligence, such as visual perception, speech recognition, decision-making. The Turing Test is a method that is a reference for determining whether or not a computer is capable of thinking like a human being.

AI is highly topical today and subject of critical debate about its societal impact and ethics. Here we reference Microsoft's submitted written evidence to the House of Lords Select Committee on AI.

The human-centered approach to AI that Microsoft envisions can only be realized if relevant stakeholders from industry, government, civil society and the research community collaborate on the development of shared principles to shape the use of AI technologies.

Microsoft's CEO, Satya Nadella, shared some initial thoughts on what these may be in order to start this dialogue. We believe that AI should:

1. Be designed to assist humanity;
2. Be transparent;

3. Maximize efficiencies without destroying the dignity of people;
4. Be designed for privacy;
5. Have algorithmic accountability so that humans can undo unintended harm;
6. Guard against bias.

Full report (1600 pages) at *https://www.parliament.uk/documents/lords-committees/Artificial-Intelligence/AI-Written-Evidence-Volume.pdf*

BAU

Business As Usual. In a world that is seemingly under assault from constant change, BAU is getting harder to define as a steady state of affairs. Perhaps BAU is really all about the acceptance of change.

Big Data

Big Data is characterized by extremely large data sets that may be analyzed computationally to reveal patterns, trends, and associations.

It is well known that we are in the midst of a data explosion and Big Data is about how that data will be processed to extract its value, some say providing insights that will bring change to the way we run business and society. It also needs people who can interpret the data and therein lies a current skills shortage.

Business Model

Not to be confused with Business Operating Model. The Business Model describes the way the business generates value and the raison d'être of their existence. Many businesses fail when their business model becomes out of date and others steal their customers with a superior (in value) business model. There are examples in the book.

Business Operating Model

This describes the way a business structures its core processes and will vary between industry sector and businesses operating in the same industry sector. It has the potential to deliver competitive differentiation and in a modern business is reliant on technology.

DevOps

DevOps is the union of people, process, and products to enable continuous delivery of value to our end users. The contraction of "Dev" and "Ops" refers to replacing siloed Development and Operations to create multidisciplinary teams that now work together with shared and efficient practices and tools. Essential DevOps practices include agile planning, continuous integration, continuous delivery, and monitoring of applications.

Source: *https://docs.microsoft.com/en-us/azure/devops/what-is-devops*

Digital Operating Model

The Digital Operating Model is where everyone comes together, Business teams, Developers, IT Operations. It's where discussions about 'digital at the core' of delivering business outcomes get turned into actionable plans. Those actionable plans become the end to end blueprint of what you are and how you operate as a digital business with change as the only constant.

Infrastructure as a Service (IaaS)

The capability provided to the consumer is to provision processing, storage, networks, and other fundamental computing resources where the consumer is able to deploy and run arbitrary software, which can include operating systems and applications. The consumer does not manage or control the underlying cloud infrastructure but has control over operating systems, storage, and deployed applications; and possibly limited control of select networking components (e.g., host firewalls).

Source: *https://nvlpubs.nist.gov/*

IT Operating Model (ITOM)

Depending on the size of your organization and reliance on IT the ITOM may be documented in a few pages or in volumes of documents. The ITOM aligns the business strategy with the day-to-day operations of IT. It is known to few people at the heart of IT operations. There are plenty of disagreements about the definition of an ITOM. One thing is for sure, if you ask 10 employees what the ITOM is, you will probably get ten blank faces. Ask them what they use the Internet for, and you will likely have a long conversation.

Machine Learning (ML)

This book makes many references to Artificial Intelligence (AI). Sometimes there is confusion about the difference between AI and ML. ML is where a machine learns to perform a specific task without using explicit instructions, relying on patterns and inference instead. It is seen as a subset of Artificial Intelligence.

Own and Operate

Many moons ago the option to acquire IT was to own and operate and staff an IT department. There remains much investment in IT hardware and software on the books of businesses being written down. The Cloud provides an economic alternative to the capital intensive own and operate model.

Platform as a Service (PaaS)

The capability provided to the consumer is to deploy onto the cloud infrastructure consumer-created or acquired applications created using programming languages, libraries, services, and tools supported by the provider. The consumer does not manage or control the underlying cloud infrastructure including network, servers, operating systems, or storage, but has control over the deployed applications and possibly configuration settings for the application-hosting environment.

Source: *https://nvlpubs.nist.gov/*

Prince 2(TM)

PRINCE2 (an acronym for **PR**ojects **IN C**ontrolled Environments) is a de facto process-based method for effective project management. Used extensively by the UK Government, PRINCE2 is also widely recognized and used in the private sector, both in the UK and internationally. The PRINCE2 method is in the public domain and offers non-proprietorial best practice guidance on project management.

Key features of PRINCE2:

- Focus on business justification
- Defined organization structure for the project management team
- Product-based planning approach
- Emphasis on dividing the project into manageable and controllable stages
- Flexibility that can be applied at a level appropriate to the project.

Source: *https://www.prince2.com/uk/what-is-prince2*

Robotic Process Automation (RPA)

In traditional workflow automation tools, a software developer produces a list of actions to automate a task and interface to the back-end system using internal application programming interfaces (APIs) or dedicated scripting language. In contrast, RPA systems develop the action list by watching the user perform that task in the application's graphical user interface (GUI), and then perform the automation by repeating those tasks directly in the GUI. This can lower the barrier to use of automation in products that might not otherwise feature APIs for this purpose.

Source: Wikipedia

Software as a Service (SaaS)

The capability provided to the consumer is to use the provider's applications running on a cloud infrastructure. The applications are accessible from various client devices through either a thin client interface, such as a web browser (e.g. web-based email), or a program interface. The consumer does not manage or control the underlying cloud infrastructure including network, servers, operating systems, storage, or even individual application capabilities, with the possible exception of limited user specific application configuration settings.

Source: *https://nvlpubs.nist.gov/*

Waterfall

The **waterfall model** is a relatively linear *sequential design* approach for certain areas of *engineering design*. In *software development*, it tends to be among the less iterative and flexible approaches, as progress flows in largely one direction ("downwards" like a *waterfall*) through the phases of conception, initiation, analysis, design, construction, testing, deployment and maintenance.

The waterfall development model originated in the *manufacturing* and *construction* industries; where the highly structured physical environments meant that design changes became prohibitively expensive much sooner in the development process. When first adopted for software development, there were no recognized alternatives for knowledge-based creative work.

Source: Wikipedia.

List of Abbreviations

Abbreviation	Description
ACL	Access Control List
ADFS	Active Directory Federation Services
ASC	Azure Security Center
AWS	Amazon Web Services
CDO	Chief Digital/Data Officer
CEO	Chief Executive Officer
CI/CD	Continuous Integration / Continuous Deployment
CIO	Chief Information Office
CISO	Chief Information Security Officer
COM	Cloud Operating Model
COTS	Commercial Off The Shelf
CSP	Cloud Solution Provider
CTO	Chief Technology Officer
DDoS	Distributed Denial of Service
DSC	Desired State Configuration
EA	Enterprise Agreement
FOM	Future Operating Model
GCP	Google Cloud Platform
GPO	Group Policy Object

Abbreviation	Description
HANA	SAP® Brand Name
HOD	Head of Delivery
HPC	High Performance Computing
IdP	Identity Provider
ITOM	Information Technology Operating Model
JML	Joiners, Movers, Leavers
JSON	JavaScript Object Notation
KPIs	Key Performance Indicators
LSP	Licensing Service Provider
MTP	Microsoft Threat Protection
NIST	National Institute of Standards and Technology
NoSQL	No SQL
NPS	Net Promoter Score
OOB	Out of the Box
PCI DSS	Payment Card Industry Data Security Standard
REST	Representational state transfer
ROI	Return on Investment
RRP	Recommended Retail Price

Abbreviation	Description
SAP S4	SAP® Brand Name
SDLC	Software Development Lifecycle Management
SIAM	Service Integration and Management
SKU	Stock Keeping Unit
SLA	Service Level Agreement
SOAP	Structured Object Access Protocol
SSO	Single Sign-on
TFS	Team Foundation Server
TOGAF	The Open Group Architecture Framework
UAT	User Acceptance Testing
ULA	User Level Agreement
VLA	Value Level Agreement
VM	Virtual Machine
VPN	Virtual Private Network

List of Abbreviations

List of Figures

Getting Involved

The Smart Questions community

There may be questions that we should have asked but didn't. Or specific questions which may be relevant to your situation, but not everyone in general. Go to the website for the book and post the questions. You never know, they may make it into the next edition of the book. That is a key part of the Smart Questions Philosophy.

Send us your feedback

We love feedback. We prefer great reviews, but we'll accept anything that helps take the ideas further. We welcome your comments on this book.

We'd prefer email, as it's easy to answer and saves trees. If the ideas worked for you, we'd love to hear your success stories. Maybe we could turn them into 'Talking Heads'-style video or audio interviews on our website, so others can learn from you. That's one of the reasons why we wrote this book. So talk to us.

feedback@smart-questions.com

Got a book you need to write?

Maybe you are a domain expert with knowledge locked up inside you. You'd love to share it and there are people out there desperate for your insights. But you don't think you are an author and don't know where to start. Making it easy for you to write a book is part of the Smart Questions Philosophy.

Let us know about your book idea, and let's see if we can help you get your name in print.

potentialauthor@Smart-Questions.com

Notes pages

We hope that this book has inspired you and that you have already scribbled your thoughts all over it. However, if you have ideas that need a little more space then please use these notes pages.

Notes pages

www.ingramcontent.com/pod-product-compliance
Lightning Source LLC
LaVergne TN
LVHW012329060326
832902LV00011B/1783